GAME *of my* LIFE
WHITE SOX

LEW FREEDMAN

SP
SPORTS
PUBLISHING
L.L.C.

SportsPublishingLLC.com

ISBN 13: 978-1-59670-291-2

Publishers: Peter L. Bannon and Joseph J. Bannon Sr.
Senior managing editor: Susan M. Moyer
Developmental editor: Doug Hoepker
Art director: Dustin J. Hubbart

Sports Publishing L.L.C.
804 North Neil Street
Champaign, IL 61820
Phone: 1-877-424-2665
Fax: 217-363-2073
SportsPublishingLLC.com

Printed in the United States of America

Library of Congress Cataloging-in-Publication Data

Freedman, Lew.
  Game of my life. White Sox : memorable stories of Chicago White Sox baseball / Lew Freedman.
    p. cm.
  ISBN 978-1-59670-291-2 (alk. paper)
  1. Chicago White Sox (Baseball team) 2. Baseball players--United States--Anecdotes. I. Title. II. Title: White Sox. III. Title: Memorable stories of Chicago White Sox baseball.
  GV875.C58F739 2008
  796.357'640977311--dc22
                        2008012464

CONTENTS

ACKNOWLEDGMENTS

The author would like to thank the Chicago White Sox organization for its help, especially officials in the communications department, Scott Reifert and Bob Beghtol.

In addition, thanks go to Tim Wiles and the library staff at the National Baseball Hall of Fame Library in Cooperstown, N.Y.

A big thank you goes to all of the current and former White Sox players, managers and coaches who cooperated with interviews telling some of the highlight stories of their Major League baseball careers.

INTRODUCTION

The Chicago White Sox are a pillar franchise of the American League. They go back to the beginning, in 1901, when the league was formed in order to compete with the National League. Charles Comiskey was the team's founder, his name adorning the outside of the ballpark for 80 years, while one of his descendents had their name on the owner's office for nearly six decades.

The dichotomy between "old" baseball teams and expansion teams isn't quite as pronounced as it is in the National Hockey League, where the names of six original franchises are invoked. Still, the Major League clubs have longer histories, naturally, and a more ingrained tradition.

This makes the White Sox one of baseball's special teams, with Chicagoans following the Sox for generations. Rooting interests are passed on like family heirlooms. At one time, the division between White Sox and Cubs fans (Chicago being blessed as one of the rare places harboring two teams) was a simple matter of geography. If you grew up on the South Side you cheered for the Sox. Allegiance is not quite so easily defined these days, but the White Sox are first in the hearts of millions of Chicago area residents.

Sox fans have several things in common. They recall team lore, being introduced to it by family members when they were young or by reading history books. They cringe at the mention of the Black Sox Scandal, the worst professional sports scandal of all time. They revere the Go-Go White Sox of the 1950s—particularly the 1959 team that brought a World Series to Comiskey Park for the first time in 40 years, thanks to Luis Aparicio, Nellie Fox, Billy Pierce, and Early Wynn.

And they still bask in the glow of the 2005 world champion White Sox, led by manager Ozzie Guillen. It had been 88 years since the World Series title belonged to the White Sox and the fans who turned out a million or so strong for a downtown parade still celebrate the achievement.

The White Sox featured many stars through the years. Many of them have passed away. They cannot speak for themselves about the game of their life, the best they ever played, the game most meaningful to them.

An astute fan gazing at the roster of the 30 White Sox included in this collection might be surprised to see the names of Big Ed Walsh and Luke Appling. Yes, old age claimed them long ago, but these two gentlemen left behind enough record of their feelings about the "game of their life" in old newspaper clippings tucked away in the archives of the National Baseball Hall of Fame to join the list of 28 other living White Sox players or team officials.

Time flies, even for fans, and some of the White Sox speaking about their chosen game are in their 80s now. Others are still playing, still wearing the crisp whites of the Sox. Regardless of era, it was a pleasure to listen to them all.

—Lew Freedman

CHAPTER 1

BIG ED WALSH

Ed Walsh is almost a mythological figure of White Sox lore. His is a name that shows up in the fine print of record books and media guides with nearly unfathomable numbers next to it. By all statistical measures, Walsh is the greatest pitcher in the history of the team, but he played for the American League so long ago that there is no one alive today who saw him throw. Still, the numbers alone leave the reader agog, especially in a modern era when starting pitchers simply do not throw complete games and are in five-man rotations. Ed Walsh was the antithesis of the modern pitcher. In 1908, Walsh's record was 40-15. He threw an astounding 464 innings and his earned run average was 1.42.

Walsh was born in Plains, Pennsylvania, in 1881 and came of age as a pitcher in nearby Wilkes-Barre. His father, Michael, was from Dublin. Walsh grew to 6-foot-1 and 193 pounds—at the time, large enough for him to be labeled "Big Ed." When he was 11, Walsh, the youngest of 13 children, dropped out of school and spent the next nine years steering mules that pulled wagons hauling coal. Walsh had more than a passing acquaintanceship with the hardscrabble life the pick and axe coal miners lived, but by the time he was 19 his primary responsibility was pitching. His right arm's magical properties rescued Walsh from a lifetime of hard labor. Between turns on the mound he also played third base and outfield to make use of his hitting skills.

When the coal industry underwent another strike in 1902, Walsh joined the more prominent Wilkes-Barre Black Diamonds in the Pennsylvania State League.

The team folded quickly, however, and Walsh migrated to Scranton, then back to Wilkes-Barre. With each team financially strapped, Walsh made little money. He floated to the Connecticut League and began perfecting his technique. Connecticut was good to Walsh. He met his wife, Rose Mary Kearney, there in 1904 and earned $125 a month for his work on the diamond. After a transfer to Newark for the International League, a White Sox scout spotted him. Charles Comiskey paid $750 for his rights.

Then, as now, the speed of a man's fastball was the main weapon that scouts noticed. Walsh's speedball was more than adequate. However, at White Sox spring training in Marlin Springs, Texas, in 1904, Walsh came into contact with an influence that changed his pitching life. His roommate was Elmer Stricklett, a short-term journeyman Major Leaguer. Stricklett showed Walsh how to throw a spitter, and in time Walsh became one of the game's most accomplished practitioners of hurling the wet one.

Walsh saw sporadic White Sox action that year, finishing 6-3. His experience was similar the next season, when he compiled an 8-3 record. The youthful Walsh, also known as "Moose," was establishing himself. He worked on the spitter but couldn't yet control it, so in game situations he used it sparingly.

In 1906 his long-term experimentation with the spitter paid off. After two seasons of hard work with the tricky pitch, Walsh had the confidence to throw it regularly and in tight situations. That year he won 17 games and was on his way to becoming the Hall of Fame-caliber pitcher Walsh is remembered as. The spitter evolved into Walsh's signature pitch, and the more he used it the better he threw it.

"I had such control of my spitter," he said years later, "that I could hit a tack on a wall with it."

Walsh blossomed and earned admirers throughout the game. Some referred to him as possessing an "iron arm" because of the number of games he started—49 in 1908—or the number of innings he threw. At a time when ballplayers were lucky to earn a few thousand dollars annually, *The Baseball Magazine* called Walsh's appendage "the $100,000 arm."

THE SETTING

By 1907, with his new pitch baffling batters, Walsh had made a name for himself. He won 24 games, pitched just over 422 innings and was getting rave reviews. All of which was impressive, but nothing could prepare the baseball world for his stupendous follow-up season.

The summer of 1908 was the height of Ed Walsh's pitching life. He led the American League in nine categories. His 40 wins represent the second-greatest number of victories during a single season in baseball history. He threw 11 shutouts, completed 42 games, and led the league in strikeouts with 269. His winning percentage was .727. Walsh's 464 innings remains a post-1900 single-season record, and the 2007 National Baseball Hall of Fame yearbook quotes him with an interesting perspective: "Although I worked hard in the mines, I work harder when I play ball."

While Walsh was throwing his heart out in 1908, three teams—his White Sox, the Detroit Tigers, and the Cleveland Indians—vied for the pennant. Entering the final days of the season, any of them could have claimed the American League title.

On October 2, 1908, Walsh took the mound for a scheduled appearance against Cleveland. The Indians were throwing Addie Joss, a remarkable right-handed hurler whose life tragically ended three years later at age 31.

This would turn out to be the greatest pitching day of Joss' career. In the heat of the pennant race, Joss tossed a perfect game against the White Sox. Walsh struck out 15 batters in a four-hit, 1-0 loss. The only run scored came in the third inning on a single, a two-base throwing error on an attempted steal, and a passed ball.

Joss' phenomenal performance aside, this was all a prelude to Walsh's most memorable effort—one day later.

THE GAME OF MY LIFE
BY BIG ED WALSH

(AS TOLD TO FRANCIS J. POWERS, *THE CHICAGO DAILY NEWS*)

CHICAGO WHITE SOX VS. CLEVELAND INDIANS, OCTOBER 3, 1908

Did you ever see Larry Lajoie bat? No. Then you have missed something. I want to tell you that there was one of the greatest hitters—and fielders, too—ever in baseball. There's no telling the records he would have made if he hit against the lively ball. To tell you about my greatest day, I'll have to go back there to October 1908, when I fanned Larry with the bases full and the White Sox' chances for the pennant hanging on every pitch to the big Frenchman.

That was October 3, and the day after I had that great game with Addie Joss, and he beat me 1-0 with a perfect game—no runs, no hits, no man reached first. There was a great pitcher and a grand fellow, Addie. That game was a surprise to both of us, for we were sitting on a tarpaulin talking about having some singing in the hotel that night, when Lajoie—he managed Cleveland—and (White Sox manager) Fielder Jones told us to warm up. A pitcher never knew when he'd work in those days.

I didn't think there'd ever be another pennant race like there was in the American League that year. All summer, four teams—the Sox, Cleveland, Detroit, and St. Louis (Browns)—had been fighting and three of 'em still had a chance on this day. When Joss beat me the day before, it left us two and a half games behind the Tigers and two behind the Naps (Cleveland). And we had only four games left to play.

It was a Saturday, and the biggest crowd ever to see a game in Cleveland up to that date jammed around the park. Jones started Frank Smith for us and we got him three runs off Glenn Liebhardt and were leading by two going into the seventh. I was down in the bullpen, ready for anything because, as I said, we had to win this one.

As I recall it, George Perring, the shortstop, was first up for Cleveland and he went all the way to second when Patsy Dougherty muffed his fly in the sun. I began to warm up in a hurry. Nig Clarke batted for Liebhardt and fanned, and things looked better. Smith would have been out of trouble, only Jesse Tannehill fumbled Josh Clarke's grounder and couldn't make a play. Clarke stole second and that upset Smith, so he walked Bill Bradley.

I rushed to the box and the first batter I faced was Bill Hinchman. Bill wasn't a champion hitter, but he was a tough man in a pinch. I knew his weakness was a spitball on the inside corner, so I told Sully (catcher Billy Sullivan) we'd have to get in close on him. And I did. My spitball nearly always broke down, and I could put it about where I wanted. Bill got a piece of the ball and hit a fast grounder that Tannehill fielded with one hand and we forced Perring at the plate.

So there were two out and Larry at bat. Now if the Frenchman had a weakness it was a fastball high and right through the middle. If you pitched inside to him, he'd tear a hand off the third baseman and if you pitched outside, he'd knock down the second baseman.

I tried him with a spitball that broke to the inside and down. You know a spitball is heavy and travels fast. Lajoie hit the pitch hard down the third base line and it traveled so fast that it curved 20 feet, I'd guess, over the foul line and into the bleachers. There was strike one.

My next pitch was a spitter on the outside, and Larry swung and tipped it foul back to the stands. Sully signed for another spitter, but I just stared at him. I never shook him off with a nod or anything like that. He signed for the spitter twice more, but I still just looked at him. Then Billy walked out to the box.

"What's the matter?" Bill asked me.

"I'll give him a fast one," I said.

Billy was dubious. Finally, he agreed.

I threw Larry an overhand fastball that raised and he watched it come over without even an offer. "Strike three!" roared (umpire) Silk O'Loughlin. Lajoie sort of grinned at me and tossed his bat toward the bench without a word.

That was the high spot of my baseball days—fanning Larry in the clutch, without him even swinging.

GAME RESULTS

The final score was 3-2 in favor of the White Sox. However, the Tigers swooped in and swiped the pennant, finishing with a 90-63 record. The Indians placed second with a 90-64 mark. And the White Sox finished 88-64.

Napoleon "Larry" Lajoie played 21 years in the majors with a .338 lifetime average, and for several years the Indians were known as the "Naps," in his honor. Lajoie was elected to the Hall of Fame in 1937.

Besides the play-by-play account given to the *Chicago Daily News*, Walsh told other reporters that his strikeout of Lajoie was "the game out of which I got the greatest thrill during my baseball career."

He noted elsewhere that "my control wasn't very good, in as much as I had had little time to warm up."

Walsh's other credits include pitching a no-hitter in 1911 and winning both games of a doubleheader twice.

Decades later he spoke to famed *New York Post* sports columnist Jimmy Cannon about another day in his career that rated highly: a game between the White Sox and the Philadelphia Athletics, played in 1911. In that game, Walsh struck out the heart of the A's order—Stuffy McInnis, Eddie Collins, and Frank "Home Run" Baker—on nine pitches. In another relief appearance, Walsh was summoned into the game with the bases loaded and nobody out.

Zip, zip, zip, strike, strike, strike. Three straight batters failed to put a bat on Walsh's pitches.

"Not a foul," Walsh said. "They didn't even get a foul off me."

REFLECTING ON BASEBALL

Walsh was in his prime during the height of the deadball era, but even with that caveat he posted remarkable numbers. In 14 seasons—all but one with the White Sox—Walsh's career ERA was 1.82. His final win-loss record was 195-126, for a winning percentage of .607. Only Jack Chesbro's 41 wins exceeded Walsh's single-game season best of 40. It's a figure that is unlikely to ever be approached again.

Walsh retired from baseball in 1917, his arm worn out from the tremendous number of innings thrown. The spitball was banned from baseball in 1920, and during the following years Walsh preached against that ruling to interviewers who asked him what he thought about his out pitch being exiled. He resented it mightily.

"Unsanitary, my foot," Walsh said once. "You didn't slobber on the ball."

Walsh was definitely a creature of baseball's deadball era and said many times that he thought the ball in play in later years was juiced too much.

"The ball is still too lively," he said in 1940. "It's a golf ball and a mighty dangerous one. There is only one thing I haven't seen yet, and that is to see a pitcher taken off the mound in a box. Teams have no infields today. They have two outfields, because what was the infield now plays back on the green."

Walsh returned to the majors for one season as an American League umpire, then rejoined the White Sox for a few different stints as coach. His son, also named Ed Walsh, played ball for him at Notre Dame and then got his own chance at the majors. The younger Walsh's lifetime record was only 11-24 in four years of play.

After he left baseball, Walsh lived all but the last few of his years in Connecticut, though after his induction in the Hall of Fame he was a regular summer visitor to the annual ceremonies in Cooperstown. He signed thousands of autographs, once estimating that he got 30,000 requests a year.

In 1958, the White Sox celebrated Ed Walsh Day at Comiskey Park after learning he had fallen on hard times, both financially (he made $3,500 in his historic 1908 season) and physically. Suffering from severe arthritis, Walsh appeared at the event in a wheelchair. Among the White Sox legends present were Red Faber, Ray Schalk, and Ted Lyons. As the honors poured in and speeches about his greatness were uttered, Walsh fought back tears.

Mayor Richard J. Daley mentioned that he was old enough to see Walsh pitch.

"You were a great one," he said.

Walsh kept his own remarks short, but his most memorable comment came from the heart. "This day I'll remember as long as I live," he said. Then he threw out the first pitch to his old catcher Schalk, though the toss was only five feet instead of the standard 60.

Walsh succumbed to cancer the next year in Florida at age 78.

CHAPTER 2

JIM LANDIS

Jim Landis is a California guy whose dad, Jim Landis Sr., was his biggest booster. They tossed a ball constantly, and his father always offered encouragement.

"Oh, god, yeah, we played catch a lot," Landis said.

But there were also rules in the Landis household about being home when supper was placed on the table. Landis didn't always make it.

"We'd be out there on the vacant lot playing baseball, and many a time I got spanked for not being home in time for dinner," Landis recalled.

Landis and his dad shared a love of all sports in northern California.

"He took me to a lot of things," Landis recalled. "We went into Oakland. They had professional fights and we were there almost every Wednesday. I love boxing. I love boxing's good old days. There weren't many big athletes in my family, but my dad was a boxer for a while. To tell you the truth, for a time, my dad's favorite sport—and mine—was ice hockey.

"I didn't get close to playing on a pond or anything like that, but at least once a week my dad would take me to a Pacific Coast League hockey game."

For all his rooting interest in area sports teams, Landis thought of himself as a baseball player first. When he was eight, his mother, Maida, sewed him the baseball uniform he used to play in local summer leagues. He entertained fanciful thoughts about one day becoming a big leaguer.

"I dreamed of it," Landis said. "It sounds silly that my mom made me a baseball uniform, but I always wore that to the field and to play."

Landis was a good player growing up in youth leagues, in high school, and at Contra Costa Junior College. Despite his talents, Landis did not realize how closely professional teams were watching him when he enrolled in the two-year school. He did not even spend a full school year at Contra Costa before the White Sox called.

"I think a term and part of another," Landis said. "Oh heck, I bet it wasn't even 10 games that we played at the junior college before I signed. I don't even know how they found me. There was no draft. I had a little bit of an inkling there was interest. On this particular day a scout for the White Sox approached me and asked me if I would sign and I said, 'Why not?'"

Since Landis wanted to play pro, the decision to leave was easy for him. He had always been one of the best players around, and now he would find out if he could compete in a bigger pond.

THE SETTING

Landis was 23 when he made the White Sox roster for the 1957 season. He was a gazelle in centerfield, tracking down anything hit into his neighborhood, but he was weak at bat. He hit only .212 and sportswriters constantly questioned manager Al Lopez as to why he kept Landis in the lineup.

Years later, Landis admitted being in awe of the situation and that it took him a while to get comfortable.

Although Landis' playing weight is listed at 180 pounds by the *Baseball Encyclopedia*, to reach such a weight he had to be wearing shoes, clothing, carrying his bat and glove, and perhaps hiding five-pound dumbbells in his pockets. He was actually about 165 when he reached the majors. At one point, Landis went on a reverse diet to gain weight that involved drinking as many as three chocolate malts a day.

Lopez stuck with Landis and it paid off in the long run. Landis' brilliant fielding acted as counterbalance to his weak hitting. He stole singles and doubles from the opposition and was such a renowned fielder that he appeared in baseball glove ads.

One quarter-page newspaper ad extolling Landis' fielding and dependence on MacGregor's great glove read: "'MacGregor's Fabulous Field Master! Grabs and holds anything I can get to!' says Jim Landis, fleet Chicago White Sox outfielder. And speedy Jim, member of MacGregor's staff of champions, can get to plenty of ill-fated near hits!" The ad included a small cartoon baseball player back-handing a zipping line drive and saying in a word bubble, "I do the running and the Field Master does the rest!"

Landis was a man of very few errors. He fielded .993 in 1959, the year the White Sox won their first pennant since the Black Sox Scandal of 1919. He also raised his average to a respectable .272, a vindication of Lopez's faith. The White Sox had last won the World Series in 1917 with a well-balanced team that featured excellent pitching, fielding, and timely hitting. "Shoeless" Joe Jackson, Ed Cicotte, Red Faber, Ray Schalk, and Eddie Collins were key figures on the superior team. Heavily favored over the Cincinnati Reds in 1919, the White Sox threw the World Series. Eight men were suspended for life and the club went into a tailspin that lasted decades. With few exceptions under the direction of manager Jimmie Dykes, the White Sox played bad baseball until the 1950s. The rejuvenated Go-Go White Sox were in the thick of the pennant race nearly every year, and when the White Sox finally captured the American League pennant after 40 years, clinching the title on a road trip to Cleveland, the players and city celebrated.

"In our day," Landis said, "when you were young, that was your dream, to be in a World Series more than anything else. You thought about it all of the time. When it happened and we clinched the pennant, there was so much jubilation. Not just by me, but everybody. Norm Cash, Bob Shaw, Barry Latman, and myself, when we got off the plane in Chicago, let's just say we took our time getting home to our wives."

The plane bringing the White Sox home landed in the early morning. Mayor Richard J. Daley, a lifelong fan of the team, had given permission for air raid sirens to be set off in celebration. Thousands of long-deprived White Sox fans showed up.

"I was shocked by how many people were at the airport at that time of night," Landis said. "It was late. And it was at least four or five in the morning before we knocked on our own doors. It wasn't even because we liked to drink, it was just the feeling about what happened."

Players live in the present. As the 1959 team closed in on the pennant, sportswriters and fans constantly reminded them how long the city had suffered without a league championship. But none of that really crossed the players' minds until the deed was accomplished.

"We never paid much attention to [the four-decade gap]," Landis said. "I was in my own era and I did the best I could. We were fortunate to win a pennant. That other stuff never really sunk into my head."

THE GAME OF MY LIFE
BY JIM LANDIS

CHICAGO WHITE SOX VS. LOS ANGELES DODGERS, WORLD SERIES GAME 1, OCTOBER 1, 1959

Sometimes when you're sitting around for a few days, I don't want to say the edge wears off . . . but all that nervousness was just as strong for us when we started performing in the first game. I thought it was a good thing. I don't know how anybody else felt, but I was still young and though not quite a rookie, still at a young stage as a player.

We felt pretty good about ourselves when the World Series started at Comiskey Park against the Dodgers. There was a lot of excitement. It did feel different waking up that morning and going to the ballpark. There was a different atmosphere.

We were a very good fielding team. Pitcher Billy Pierce always said we had strength up the middle. He meant Nellie Fox at second base and Luis Aparicio at shortstop. He included me in centerfield and that was nice, but those other two were Hall of Famers. They were both tremendous. I used to be in awe of them, standing behind them in the field.

During the season we were not a big-hitting team. Bill Veeck became the owner that year and it seemed as if he spent the whole season trying to find another power hitter. Then, near the end of the season, he got Ted Kluszewski. He was a huge guy who liked to show off his muscles. He ripped the sleeves off his uniform.

We came out in the first game of the World Series and we played about as perfectly as you can. We won 11-0 and Kluszewski hit two home runs. In a lot of ways we thought we were on our way. I'm not saying we got cocky or anything like that, but we just said, "Hey, we won the first one, we've got a darned good chance now."

Winning it big was even more encouraging. I had a good day that day, which makes it all the better since it was a first World Series game.

GAME RESULTS

Early Wynn, the stalwart right-hander who won the Cy Young Award for his 22-victory season, pitched seven strong innings in the opener, surrendering six hits. Gerry Staley pitched two effective innings of relief. Big Klu stroked two two-run homers and a single for five RBIs. Landis himself had an amazing day, collecting three hits in four at-bats, scoring three runs and driving in one. Alas, for White Sox fans, the Series had reached a peak. This was the first World Series the Dodgers played in after their departure from Brooklyn, and the new ballpark going up at Chavez Ravine was not ready for occupancy, so the West Coast games were played in the Los Angeles Coliseum.

The Coliseum was one of the oddest stadiums used for baseball any time after 1920. The mammoth stadium was built for football and is still used for that today. It was loosely adapted for Dodger baseball. The weirdest feature was its short left-field wall, only 252 feet from home plate. It was a friendly invitation for right-handed batters, and for anyone who could hit a pop-up. Depending on the time of day games—World Series games were not scheduled at night in 1959—the sun was also often in fielders' faces.

Landis hated the L.A. Coliseum. "It wasn't a ballpark, for God's sake," he said. "It was for football. It was weird. It was tough to pick up a ball (a fly off the bat) because the damned sun was right there. I lost a ball in the sun."

Landis' instincts were usually as sharp as a homing pigeon's. He never misjudged fly balls, so it is not surprising that nearly 50 years later he still holds a grudge against the Coliseum.

"That's why it was embarrassing in a World Series game," he said. "I don't remember another time I dropped an easy fly ball. It was horrible."

The White Sox lost game two to the Dodgers in Chicago and fell behind 3-1 before succumbing in six games. The Sox would not appear in another World Series until 2005.

REFLECTING ON BASEBALL

Jim Landis is lucky he can remember anything about the 1959 World Series. In the fourth inning of the sixth game, Landis caught a Johnny Podres pitch in the head. The incident knocked Landis to the ground as fans in Comiskey Park quieted after the explosive sound of the ball hitting Landis' batting helmet. The rising inside fastball caught Landis off-guard. He said he was planning to take a strike and was too relaxed at the plate. When he spun to duck away from the pitch, it was too late.

"I know he wasn't throwing at me," Landis said at the time. "It hurt. I was momentarily stunned. It left a pretty good-sized lump. I told him there were no ill feelings. I explained it was probably my fault."

Landis chose not to leave the game, though he could feel evidence of the collision for some time afterward.

Landis said one regular-season catch off Dick Williams, then a utility man for the Kansas City Athletics, might be the best he ever made.

"It was a darned good catch where I was coming in and diving," Landis said. "The ball was a line drive in front of me and it saved Billy Pierce the ballgame."

The hit was a sinking line drive. He ran in, dove straight ahead, and speared the ball about two inches off the ground. The next day, Williams came up to him and said, "God damn you."

Landis asked what was the matter.

He said, "That would have been the first hit I got off of Billy Pierce, and you took it away from me. I'll always remember that."

When Landis retired from major league baseball after the 1967 season he returned to California and spent close to two decades working for a friend's safety sign business. He missed baseball, though more the interaction with teammates than play on the field.

"For me, they were a great bunch of guys—Billy Pierce, Nellie Fox, Jim Rivera," he said. "In our day, on the road maybe seven or eight guys would go out to dinner together. I missed the game, but I missed the guys more."

From afar, Landis has continued to root for the White Sox. One of his sons is a professional sports agent and even represents two prominent members of the modern Sox: first baseman Paul Konerko and pitcher Jon Garland. Landis stays in touch with the White Sox, especially when something good happens to a former teammate. In 1997, when Nellie Fox was posthumously inducted into the National Baseball Hall of Fame, Landis attended the ceremony in Cooperstown, New York.

"Nellie was a great guy and a great ballplayer," Landis told the *Chicago Tribune* at the time. "He was the glue that kept us together."

Landis saw two White Sox World Series games in 2005, and in 2007 he was present at U.S. Cellular Field when the team unveiled a statue of Billy Pierce in the outfield. He may live in California, but Jim Landis is still a member of the White Sox extended family.

CHAPTER 3

GERRY STALEY

Gerry Staley lived in Washington state his whole life until his death in January of 2008 at age 87. He began playing semi-pro baseball in high school in the late 1930s under the influence of his older brothers: Roy, an infielder, and Joe, a southpaw pitcher.

"I just followed what they did," Staley said. "They were better ballplayers than me."

Better at the time, perhaps, but they didn't advance in the game the way Staley did, despite his conviction that hard-throwing Joe could have made the big time.

"The only thing that held him back," Staley recalled, "was that he was married and he couldn't make enough money to play."

After graduating high school, Staley went to work at an aluminum plant in Vancouver. He became friends with another worker who also had a baseball background and told him he was going to leave the job to manage a team in Boise, Idaho.

"He wanted to know if there were any ballplayers or prospects living around there," Staley said.

Boise was a Class C club in the Pioneer League and a former Pacific Coast League regular named Jim Keesey invited Staley to spring training.

In his first season with Boise in 1940, Staley made $100 a month and won 22 games. Any player who produced that well in the minors today would be gobbled up by a major-league franchise, but there were hundreds of minor league teams and Boise was out of the mainstream. Staley returned for a second year and won 20 games. By then he was making $125 a month.

"They gave me a big raise of $25," Staley chuckled.

As soon as Staley packed away his glove, he returned to Vancouver to work in a sawmill started by brother Joe. Staley and his wife, Shirley, were raising a son and a daughter, so the off-season income was necessary. Later, because of his affiliation with the sawmill, sportswriters occasionally referred to Staley as "The Lumberjack."

It was obvious after winning 42 games in two seasons that Staley was too good for Class C competition and deserved a chance at a higher level of play, but then the Japanese bombed Pearl Harbor, so Staley spent the next three years in the military. After the war, he wanted to resume his baseball career and soon discovered that his Boise seasons had been noticed. The AAA Sacramento Solons (affiliated with the St. Louis Cardinals) had been eyeing Staley.

"They had the chance to select one player from the service list," Staley said. "Well, they selected me and I went to spring training with the Cardinals in 1947."

Under Branch Rickey, the Cardinals had been in the forefront of developing minor league talent, studying players by the hundreds and trying to keep all the best ones for themselves. Staley was no young rookie, turning 27 that year, but he made it into a Cardinals uniform long enough to finish 1-0.

In mid-season, Staley was shipped to AAA Columbus, Ohio, where he won a handful of games and almost pitched Columbus into the postseason. Staley threw a knuckler and a sinker, but his greatest success was being spotted in spring training in 1948 by future Cardinals Hall of Famer Red Schoendienst's brother, Julius Schoendienst, who suggested that Staley alter his motion to throw three-quarters instead of overhand.

Staley was in the majors to stay, spending eight seasons with the Cardinals, mostly as a starter. He won a career-high 19 games in 1951 and added 17 victories in 1952 and 18 in 1953. After a losing season in 1954, Staley moved on to Cincinnati, then the New York Yankees, and finally ended up with the Chicago White Sox before the end of the 1956 season, where he finished with an 8-3 record. The combination of significant wins as a starter and a fair share of saves parallels the career of Hall of Famer Dennis Eckersley.

By 1957, Staley was immersed in the second phase of his Major League career as a full-time reliever, and in 1959 he was the Sox's most dependable man out of the pen, making 67 appearances. He played a huge role in the White Sox's run to the World Series.

THE SETTING

The Chicago White Sox had not won a pennant since 1919, when the team that will live in infamy for fixing the World Series conquered the American League during the regular season. The 1950s Sox had been on the rise, improving under managers Paul Richards, Marty Marion, and Al Lopez. Each season the club tinkered with personnel, added new faces, juggled the lineup and moved closer to having the core required to out-race the Yankees for the league crown. Before the start of the 1959 season, for the second time in three years, Lopez announced that the Yankees could be had.

Staley teamed with Turk Lown to give the White Sox a one-two bullpen punch that few teams could match. Unlike present-day baseball where the jobs of long relievers, set-up men, and closers are clearly defined, in the 1950s there were only relief pitchers. Men like Staley might face a single batter or pitch three innings.

That season, long before complete games became virtually extinct, Staley won eight games out of the bullpen and saved 14 others. The Yankees weren't even viable candidates for the pennant. The true competition was the Cleveland Indians.

As the season wound down, slumping Chicago led Cleveland by 3½ games in the standings. The White Sox traveled to Cleveland for a critical September series and lost the first two games by one run each. Lopez had overextended his pitching staff. Thus, there was much at stake when Staley—39 and in the twilight of his career—came in to pitch one of the most satisfying appearances of his life and one of the most important in White Sox history.

THE GAME OF MY LIFE
BY GERRY STALEY

CHICAGO WHITE SOX VS. THE CLEVELAND INDIANS, SEPTEMBER 22, 1959

The biggest game of my life is the one in Cleveland. It was to end the 1959 season. We had been leading the league the whole time, but nothing was permanent. It would be nice to get it over with, but you go out and play each game day to day.

There was a big crowd there as expected, since we were in first place and the Indians were in second. I think they had more than 50,000 people. Early Wynn had started the game. He was our big-game pitcher that year. He had a wonderful season. But then he came out of the game and Bob Shaw—usually a starter—was on the mound for the ninth inning.

We were ahead 4-2. The first out came on a pop-up by Woody Held, the Indians' second baseman. But then things got a little bit tense; Jim Baxes was up next and he got a piece of a pitch, so he was safe at first with a single. Jack Harshman was up next. He was a good hitting pitcher, and he lined a single to right field. Jimmy Piersall hit Shaw's pitch hard to the right side, but Nellie Fox got his glove on it. By keeping the ball in the infield, Baxes couldn't score. So the Indians had the bases loaded.

Lopez came out to replace Shaw and brought me in. Bases loaded, one out. Vic Power, a very solid hitter, was at the plate. I threw a sinker—I was throwing almost all sinkers and knuckleballs—and Power hit it to Luis Aparicio at short. One pitch, a double play, and that gave us the pennant. We had a nice celebration afterward—not on the field, because it was their field, but in the clubhouse and on the plane back to Chicago.

GAME RESULTS

The final score was 4-2. The White Sox opened the champagne and enjoyed a sense of relief at notching a pennant for themselves and the city of Chicago. The players got an immediate reminder of just how much the championship meant to Chicagoans when their plane landed at Midway Airport: an estimated 25,000 people showed up to applaud the team, while other fans celebrated in the streets. For Staley, who had come close to first place on other occasions, capturing a pennant felt like a career capstone.

"It sure was frustrating," Staley said of the preceding years. "So it was really nice to win one. I had spent many years with different teams, and so many times it seemed we were only one or two games out of first. That game (against Cleveland) was more exciting than the others. That was a fun ride home."

Within days the White Sox were engaged in their first World Series in 40 years against the Los Angeles Dodgers. Although the Sox lost four games to two, Staley collected a win and a save in four appearances. Nearly five decades later he remembers how strange it was in the Los Angeles Coliseum.

"It was a football stadium," Staley said, "and left field was so close you could almost pee over it. I was pitching there once and Marty Marion, who was the manager in Chicago for a while, backed up on a fly from the shortstop position for the Cardinals and the doggone ball hit the overhang for a home run."

The White Sox players of the 1950s were close, had been together for a while, and were "a terrific bunch of fellows," in Staley's words. They ate up the attention and tried to give the long-time fans a World Series.

The White Sox gained confidence after their 11-0 first-game victory, a game where Staley relieved Early Wynn.

"It was a really, really big day, but one game is just one game," Staley said.

The White Sox only won one more game and ended up losing the Series.

REFLECTIONS ON BASEBALL

Gerry Staley had his best overall pitching season with the White Sox a year later, in 1960, when he finished 13-8 with 10 saves and was selected for the American League All-Star team (after twice being chosen in the National League). However, his next year, as he moved from team to team, would be his last. After Staley retired he spent one year as a coach for the Portland, Oregon minor league team and then returned to Vancouver. Besides all the memories, Staley kept scrapbooks with stories about his career and a cross-section of baseballs from games he pitched.

Back home, Staley accepted a position as superintendent of the Clark County Parks and Recreation Department and held it for 17 years. He also spent considerable time traveling by motor home. Baseball was Staley's first passion, but spending time in the outdoors was a favorite off-field pastime.

In his late 80s Staley still followed baseball closely and marveled at how much money today's players earn. The off-season job is a distant memory for current players, who instead spend their time lifting weights and conditioning. In his final years, Staley enjoyed following both the White Sox and the Cardinals on television especially with the Sox World Series win in 2004 and the Cardinals winning it in 2006. If they ever faced one another in a World Series, Staley's allegiance would have been stretched.

But the game was the thing, just as it was when he was a youth.

"Do I watch a lot of baseball?" Staley said. "What else? I like watching the teams and it gives me something to do."

When he had a free moment, Staley revisited those scrapbooks and recalled the time he clinched a pennant for Chicago with a single pitch.

CHAPTER 4

BILLY PIERCE

Billy Pierce was born in Detroit in 1927 and grew up in Highland Park, Michigan, the son of a pharmacist named John Walter Pierce who owned a drugstore for about 30 years. Pierce was a baseball fan from an early age and also rooted for University of Michigan sports. For most of his youth, Pierce was a sandlot player competing in pickup games with other neighborhood kids. Pierce got some of his baseball instincts from his father, who played high school ball, but no one else in his family participated in organized athletics. Pierce's early play was all impromptu. The kids used their equipment until it fell apart.

"It sounds corny, but we would wrap a baseball with friction tape," Pierce recollected. "We put friction tape around a bat or put a little nail in it. We played on the school grounds, we played in the alleys where a telephone pole was a base, and maybe a sewer was second base. We'd start early in the morning and play all day long."

To Pierce, the only baseball team that mattered was the Detroit Tigers and all he knew was the American League. His favorite players were Hall of Fame second baseman Charlie Gehringer and pitcher Tommy Bridges. He also enjoyed collecting baseball cards. When Pierce was in his mid-teens he and some friends formed their own team called the Owls and joined the Detroit Amateur Baseball Federation. While the nickname didn't exactly strike fear into the hearts of their opponents, the Owls were pretty good. Initially, Pierce was a first baseman, but the Owls underwent an abrupt personnel change a week before the season began.

"The boy who was supposed to be our pitcher went to another neighborhood team because they had nicer uniforms," Pierce said. "I could throw harder than anybody else, and I was wilder than anybody, so I became the pitcher. I pitched all of the games."

The Owls won a title. At 17, Pierce switched to a still-higher class and won another title. The southpaw learned to harness his fastball and continued to excel on his high school team, which won the Detroit city championship. Scouts started to take notice. Although he had fun playing baseball, Pierce never considered the sport a career prospect at the time. He had different aspirations.

"I was going to be a doctor," he said. "My dad was the head of a pharmacy, so I was around medicine a lot with different people. That was my idea through school."

Pierce was selected to play in the 1944 Esquire All-American baseball game, taking place in the Polo Grounds in New York. The honor led him to a four-year scholarship, which meshed nicely with his medical goals. Pierce, who now has a vast collection of autographed pictures on the wall of his basement, retains one of his oldest photographs from that game. The opposing managers were Hall of Fame players Mel Ott and Carl Hubbell.

Pierce was chosen Most Valuable Player in the all-star game and was given his award by legendary manager Connie Mack. Pierce has a photo of him with Mack—unfortunately unsigned, something he considers a missed opportunity.

Pierce intended to enroll at the University of Michigan and was wooed by the head baseball coach, but when the Tigers scouted him, he couldn't pass up his hometown team. In the fall of 1944, Pierce signed with the Tigers instead of attending classes in Ann Arbor. He intended to give baseball a three-year try, and if he failed he would go to college. Pierce never used the scholarship.

When Pierce was negotiating his contract in the office of Tigers' general manager Jack Zeller, the door opened and in walked Gehringer, wearing his U.S. Navy uniform.

"Looking sharp and looking great," Pierce said. "One of my idols and here he is. If I wasn't going to sign before, I was going to then, for sure. I think they set that up. I met him two or three times after that. He was just a great gentleman. Signing with the hometown team, that was the big thing. I didn't really think too much about the future—maybe that wasn't too smart. Most ballplayers go out there and give it their 100 percent, and a lot of time that will work, but sometimes it just doesn't. I've seen fellows that have the greatest hearts in the world who really wanted to play, but there was just something they didn't have. They either couldn't hit the curveball or there was just something missing, so they didn't make a great career of it."

Pierce's career began auspiciously. The Tigers won the American League pennant in 1945 when he was a rookie and kept him on the postseason roster. This was mostly just to soak up the atmosphere, because with starters like Hal Newhouser and Dizzy Trout, the 18-year-old's services were not in demand. He and another young pitcher, Art Houtteman, were only along for the ride.

"I didn't get in any games," Pierce said. "I threw batting practice. We were there and we were members of the team and eligible for the World Series, but we didn't get in. They had some pretty good pitching at that time."

After the Series, Pierce disappeared into the minors and coped with a bad back before resurfacing as a full-time Major Leaguer in 1948. Pierce was traded to the White Sox in time for the 1949 season and his career began to blossom. The winner of 15 games in 1951, Pierce was an all-star by 1953. That summer he started the first of three all-star games.

THE SETTING

The White Sox had been second-division residents of the American League for about 30 years when Pierce joined the team, but his acquisition was part of the assembly of a new team by general manager Frank Lane. Pierce was one of the cornerstone pieces of a new generation of players who grew into the Go-Go White Sox. When Pierce was selected to play in the 1953 All-Star game it was a symbol of fresh White Sox blood making an impact. Pierce's participation in a prominent role as the starting American League pitcher signified that the White Sox were on their way back.

THE GAME OF MY LIFE
BY BILLY PIERCE

MAJOR LEAGUE ALL-STAR GAME, JULY 14, 1953

When I was picked to start my first All-Star game in 1953 at Crosley Field in Cincinnati, it was a tremendous thrill. Here I am with ballplayers that I had admired and watched, and now I'm playing on the same field with them.

Crosley Field was a small park, not that impressive. The clubhouse was way out in left field and you had to walk all the way across the field to get to the dugout.

Casey Stengel was the manager because the Yankees had won the pennant the year before, and he picked me to start. In 1955 it was Al Lopez, after the Indians were in the World Series the year before, and in 1956 it was Stengel again. I was fortunate. I got to start three All-Star games. The first one is naturally the biggest. It was just a tremendous day.

The All-Star lineups were picked through fan voting, but the pitchers were picked by the managers. You can't really expect to be chosen. You never know. Maybe you didn't want to jinx yourself, but it wasn't talked about. Nowadays a fellow plays in it one year and they start writing, 'Well, he'll be in the Hall of Fame.' It's just a completely different thought process. Players have it written into their contracts that they get bonus money if they make the All-Star team.

I never associated much with the opposition when we were playing, so I didn't really know the other players. Being a pitcher, you're not running the bases and running into them all of the time. I got to know most of them better after I got out of baseball and became friends with them.

But in the All-Star game you've got Ted Williams on your team. You've got Mickey Mantle on your team. You've got Yogi Berra catching you. We had a lot of future Hall of Famers playing in that game. Stan Musial was on the other side. Just tremendous ballplayers. I was thrilled.

I pitched well in the game. The starting pitcher for the National League was Robin Roberts of the Phillies. He pitched well, too. I pitched my three innings and only gave up one hit and didn't walk anybody. Roberts also gave up one hit.

I started three All-Star games, allowed one run, and got one loss. The team lost all three games. It's funny. You pitch nine innings in All-Star games, allow one run, and you get a loss.

GAME RESULTS

The American League lost, 5-1, in the late innings, but Pierce, who became a seven-time All-Star, had little to do with the loss.

Over time, the All-Star game evolved into more of an exhibition than a contest between the leagues, and in 2006, Commissioner Bud Selig decided to add a new twist to the event. He decreed that the World Series representative of the league that wins the game would receive home-field advantage in the championship round.

Pierce won 18 games during the 1953 season and was selected for seven All-Star games. He was still a key performer on the White Sox when the team won the pennant in 1959.

"When I was a kid I lived in an American League city," Pierce said. "The only time we ever saw National League players before cable TV was the All-Star game and the World Series. They were kind of strangers."

The rarity of interleague competition was one thing that made the All-Star game stand out. There was more of a show-off quality, as players sought to prove the superiority of their league. And if your team didn't make it to the World Series, the only thing top players had was the All-Star game.

In 1959, Pierce experienced the joy of advancing to a World Series. After a decade of trying with the same team, the White Sox put it all together and captured the American League flag. The pennant-clinching moment, in a late September game at Cleveland, is as vivid for Pierce today as it was then, though he didn't play in the game.

"When we won the pennant, when Luis (Aparicio) caught the ground ball, stepped on second, and threw to first for the double play, that has to rate as one of my favorites," Pierce said. "I was warming up in the bullpen. The elation was just tremendous. There was champagne and a tremendous amount of excitement, to have that moment where we were winners."

REFLECTING ON BASEBALL

In 1955, Pierce compiled a league-leading earned run average of 1.97, the best in the majors in nine years. His win-loss record was only 15-10 because Pierce lost four 1-0 games. In 1956, his record was 20-9. In 1957, his record was 20-12. All of that was with the White Sox, but Pierce played the final few years of his career with the San Francisco Giants and put up a 16-6 mark in the team's 1962 World Series year. During his career, Pierce pitched four one-hit ballgames.

The 1959 season remains special in the hearts and minds of White Sox fans because the pennant was hard-earned and the team hadn't claimed one in so long.

"It was an all-around team," Pierce said. "We had a good defensive ballclub. We won the close ballgames. We won the one-run games—most of them—because we had a good, solid shortstop, second baseman, and centerfielder. We didn't give anything away and the hitting was fine."

Pierce won 211 games in his 18-year career and was considered such a nice guy in baseball quarters that some believed it detracted from his ability to dominate by brushing back sluggers.

Pierce's reputation as a swell guy followed him into retirement. Pierce, who has been married to his wife, Gloria, since 1949 and has raised three children, lived in Detroit throughout his playing career but relocated the family to the Chicago area just as he retired in 1964. Pierce and Gloria each have had knee replacement surgery.

"She kids me that I got mine pitching and she got hers praying that I would do well," Pierce said.

Pierce was not interested in staying in professional ball as a scout, coach, or manager, but surprised himself by becoming a Little League and Pony League coach for about 20 years starting in 1965.

"I got involved in it and I loved it," Pierce said. "I've always loved the game of baseball."

Pierce also remained close to the White Sox organization, making speeches and attending banquets for the franchise. The club retired his number 19 jersey and in the summer of 2007 unveiled a statue of him pitching.

Besides his professional business work, Pierce has been heavily involved in the Chicago Baseball Cancer Charity since 1970. He has been president and chairman as the organization raised more than $11 million for cancer research and work at Chicago hospitals. The bulk of the money has been raised through annual celebrity golf tournaments in July, featuring retired athletes.

Forever a White Sox rooter, Pierce attends a half-dozen games or so each season and is a devoted watcher of their televised games. When the White Sox won the World Series in 2005, it meant almost as much to Pierce as if he had still been active. The team did its utmost to involve ex-Sox heroes in the festivities, and Pierce threw out the first pitch in a playoff game against the Angels.

"I thought it was absolutely fantastic," Pierce said. "Here we are in a city that hasn't won a world championship in 88 years and there were so many close games that could go either way. But when you win 15 out of 16 games at the end of the year, it doesn't matter that you just barely won them. The greatest thing in the world to me was what it meant to the South Side fans, the dyed-in-the-wool White Sox fans, and the other Chicago fans. A lot of people came together for that."

CHAPTER 5

TURK LOWN

Omar "Turk" Lown—earning his nickname on account of his Turkish heritage—was born in Brooklyn in 1924 and started playing baseball when he was in elementary school. He and all of his friends in the neighborhood went to nearby playgrounds and played sports all day long.

"That's all you did," Lown recalled. "You got up in the morning in the summer time and never saw mom Mom and Dad. My older brother Bill (who passed away in 2006) and I were always at the playground playing baseball or basketball or something."

Bill was a couple of years older, so he influenced Turk with the way he used his free time.

"We did everything together," Lown said. "It wasn't that he said, 'Come on along, Turk.' We just got up and both did it. There were baseball fields all over. When I go back to the area now—Public School 88 was only a couple of blocks from where we grew up and had two big fields—I see that they're all filled in with parking spaces and extra buildings."

Lown was more of a participant than a fan, despite the proximity of the Dodgers.

"My older brother was a great baseball fan," Lown said. "With eight teams in each league he knew everybody's average, pitching records, and everything else. I didn't pay much attention to it. I had never seen a Major League game until I went into professional sports."

When Lown began playing baseball for pay, it was with the Dodgers' organization and he quickly established a connection with the Colorado mountains. Lown was assigned to the Pueblo Dodgers minor-league franchise and played the 1947 and 1948 seasons at a high altitude. This was also where he met his wife, Vi.

Although Lown didn't see National League games when he was a kid, his parents took him to games featuring Brooklyn semi-pro teams, such as the Farmers, the Grays, and the Cuban All-Stars at a ballpark called the Farmers Oval. Like many players in the 1940s, Lown's career was delayed by World War II. He was discharged from the Army in 1945 and went to Dodgers spring training in 1946. Lown's arm had gone bad and he was going to have surgery.

"I couldn't throw," he said. "But I was sitting in the dugout, a fresh-assed rookie, and Leo Durocher came in."

Durocher, the flamboyant manager of the Dodgers, made it his business to study the up-and-comers in the farm system. He chose that moment to encourage Lown in a way that let the young player know he knew all about him. "He says, 'Son, I hear you're going to get your arm done. Don't worry about it. You'll be back and there won't be any trouble at all.' I thought that was really nice of him to come over and say that." By the time Lown broke into the majors in 1951, he was property of the Chicago Cubs and went 4-9 that season. He spent most of the 1950s with the Cubs, made a short detour to Cincinnati, and before the end of the 1958 season was a member of the Chicago White Sox.

Lown became a key component of the White Sox bullpen, forming a successful partnership with Gerry Staley, as the club matured into the 1959 American League champions. Relief pitchers were employed quite differently in the 1950s than they are today. When Lown was summoned to the mound in relief, he expected to pitch one to three innings, depending on circumstances. Once in a while he was caught off-guard.

THE SETTING

In spring training, manager Al Lopez predicted that the New York Yankees could be beaten, and he felt his White Sox were ready to claim a long overdue pennant. The White Sox were positioning themselves to capture first place.

Lown bounced from the Cubs to the Reds to the White Sox in 1958, but established himself in the White Sox bullpen during the second half of that season. He finished 3-3 with 27 appearances, all in relief. Lown earned Lopez's trust, and in 1959 the duo represented the foundation of the bullpen. If Lopez didn't call on one, he called on the other. If he needed more help in a close game, Lopez called on both.

The White Sox and Lown were a perfect match at a perfect time. In 1959, the Sox made their run for the pennant and Lown turned in his finest performance. He posted a 9-2 record, appeared in 60 games, and led the American League with 15 saves.

"He did a great job of relieving that year," said teammate and fellow pitcher Billy Pierce. "That was the first time we had a really reliable relief corps."

Lown polished off most batters with his fastball, but he also possessed a blooper-type pitch that could befuddle batters. It was quite unorthodox and Lopez hated it.

"He had a pet pitch that was real slow and went up in the air," Pierce recalled. "Every time he threw it, Lopez went crazy."

Lown enjoyed the type of season where it didn't matter much what he threw, but one outing surprised him for a couple of reasons.

THE GAME OF MY LIFE
BY TURK LOWN

CHICAGO WHITE SOX VS. BALTIMORE ORIOLES, JULY 25, 1959

Every time I mention a game and talk about the White Sox, to my kids or to anyone, one game stands out in my memory when I relieved at Comiskey Park.

The game went deep into extra innings and usually Gerry Staley and I were just the late men, but I came in and stayed in the game. Al left me in, which was unusual. As each inning passed, I got more and more surprised. We were playing against the Baltimore Orioles. Billy O'Dell started for Baltimore and Bob Shaw started for us. Shaw pitched 11 innings—that wasn't that uncommon in those days. O'Dell pitched 9⅓ innings for them. The game went into extra innings at 2-2.

I relieved Shaw and pitched six innings. I gave up only three hits and struck out two. I walked only one batter. The game just kept going on. Every inning when I started to walk out there, I said, "Holy mackerel." I just kept going out there and throwing. The game finally ended in the bottom of the 17th inning.

GAME RESULTS

The White Sox won the game, 3-2, by scoring a run in the bottom of the 17th. Attendance was 12,552, though it was unclear how many stayed for the entire four hours and 35 minutes.

It was the longest relief outing of Lown's career and was later overshadowed by the White Sox team accomplishments as they steamrolled to the pennant and a place in the World Series. But Lown remembers the game with particular fondness and as a counterpoint to the way Major League managers handle their staffs in the modern game with standing-room-only crowds in the bullpen.

"I'm really surprised how they handle pitchers now," Lown said. "I follow the Colorado Rockies and there was a guy who had a shutout going into the eighth or ninth inning. There was a man on second base and the pitcher had just struck a man out and they put a relief pitcher in. The starter threw only 74 pitches. And they lost the ball game."

Complete games have become an endangered species in baseball, and "long" relief now means about two innings.

"I guess they're paying these relief pitchers so much money that they feel they have to bring them in," Lown said. "But it's ridiculous and it's a shame for the starting pitchers. Not many pitchers pitch a nine-inning ballgame any more."

Though other players had their moments, it seemed that Lown and Staley were the entire White Sox bullpen during the pennant year.

"Gerry threw the sinker ball and the knuckler and I guess Al figured that it was best to bring me in for a strikeout at a particular time because of my fastball," Lown said.

The White Sox had a roster filled with mature players. They had been believers in their abilities for several years and they recognized how pennant-hungry their fanbase was, but Lown said the team took care of business without a "gee-whiz attitude."

"We didn't have a real young ballclub. We had an older ballclub and there was nothing like an 'Oh, boy' outlook. Or, 'We've got to win this one. We're getting close. If we do, we win the pennant.' There was no talk about it whatsoever. You just went out and played the ballgame that was to be played that day."

REFLECTING ON BASEBALL

Lown said the White Sox were so matter-of-fact that at first when the team won its pennant-clinching game in Cleveland, he didn't even realize it had happened. It took only seconds for the celebration to begin, however, and he was quickly soaked with beer in the locker room.

"When it happened, it was fabulous," Lown said. "The great parade they had for us in Chicago is something I'll never forget."

The White Sox remained an all-business team in the World Series. Unlike baseball today, the ban on fraternization between teams was more strictly applied. Lown had played in the minors with Dodger first baseman Gil Hodges, but when he reached base in the Series on a bunt single, he didn't even talk to him.

"We didn't fraternize," Lown said. "You didn't see everybody standing around the batting cage laughing and having a good time. Guys (from opposing teams) are hugging in the batting cage. I told my wife one time, 'Look at that! Look at the manager out there slapping hands!' By the time we got done with the ballgame and the third out was through, my managers were in the clubhouse. Now they're all standing out there slapping each other, having a parade."

The White Sox despised the Los Angeles Coliseum.

"The shortstop was rubbing against the left-field fence," he said. "Al Smith (Sox right fielder) was so far out you could hardly see him. But you block it all out. I really thought we had a good enough ballclub to win, and with a break there and there we might have. Chuck Essegian had some big hits and nobody counted on Larry Sherry in relief. You'll find, most of the time, when a playoff or a World Series comes around, there's always some ballplayer where everything he does seems to come out right."

When Lown retired from baseball after the 1962 season, he tried a couple of jobs, but didn't like them because they kept him indoors. Then he joined the U.S. Postal Service in Pueblo and spent the next 21 years as a mail carrier. Although he still roots for the White Sox first—and happily followed them to the 2005 World Series championship—Lown watches the Colorado Rockies on television quite often as well. Occasionally, people recognize his name.

"When I say 'Turk Lown,' they say, 'Oh, did you play ball? That's nice.'"

Lown's children were all active in sports and his oldest son, Craig, signed a contract to pitch for the White Sox. His career, however, was waylaid by a rotator cuff injury. Lown's children may be happy to have a dad who was a Major Leaguer, but for Lown, when it comes to talking about the old days with the White Sox, that's mostly reserved for contacts with former teammates. Lown stayed in touch with Staley and whenever the Sox have a reunion he tries to be there.

CHAPTER 6

JIM RIVERA

Manuel Joseph "Jim" Rivera was born in 1922 and raised in New York, and though there are many famous stories about ballplayers of his generation being introduced to baseball by playing stickball in the streets, Rivera's first athletic love was altogether different.

"I was a boxer first," Rivera said.

There was a time in the United States when baseball ruled fans' hearts unequivocally, but boxing rated nearly as high on the sports allegiance meter. Rivera's upbringing was challenging; his family was poor and it was never guaranteed where each meal was coming from. Rivera, however, was a tough guy, and his toughness was eventually channelled into organized fighting.

When Rivera says that he was a boxer first, he doesn't only mean chronologically. It was his favorite sport. Rivera gravitated toward amateur boxing and twice competed in the Golden Gloves tournament as a middleweight. When he joined the Army, Rivera continued fighting in organized bouts for his unit. Yet he also picked up on baseball, motivated by something much different than the enjoyment of whacking a curveball.

"I played baseball on the weekends because if you played baseball you didn't have any KP duty," Rivera recalled. "You better believe that was the attraction. I loved baseball, but I liked boxing better. Boxing was the first mistake I made, though. I really didn't have a killer instinct."

When he was released from the service, Rivera was invited to try out for the Atlanta Crackers, a famous minor league team. He made an impression, though not enough to stick with the club. However, the owner had ties with a team in Gainesville, Florida and Rivera headed there to begin his professional baseball career. Both Rivera and the team were a hit, winning both the pennant and the playoffs. Rivera's ascension was marked by stops in Puerto Rico for winter ball and with the Seattle Rainiers in AAA in the Pacific Coast League. In 1951 his manager was Rogers Hornsby, the greatest-hitting second baseman of all time who finished his career with a .356 average. Hornsby had the reputation of a man who was difficult to get along with, but Rivera disagrees.

"No, no, no," Rivera said. "He was kind of grouchy, but he was great. If you hit .200, you played if you worked at it. But if you didn't hustle, you didn't play. I was the batting champ that year and led in stolen bases and runs scored."

While Rivera was occupying himself in Puerto Rico—his regular winter workout program—the White Sox purchased his contract. Then Hornsby became manager of the St. Louis Browns and engineered a transfer of Rivera to St. Louis, followed by Rivera's return to the White Sox. Rivera's actual Major League debut took place in 1952 with the Browns.

"After about five weeks the White Sox bought me back," Rivera said. "I was glad."

It was in the early 1950s that Rivera acquired his famous nickname, "Jungle Jim." One spring training, the White Sox were matched up in an exhibition game with the Brooklyn Dodgers. Don Newcombe, emerging as the ace of the Dodgers' pitching staff, was pitching that day. Rivera reached first base on a single right through the box and, as he had been trained to do, was on the prowl for an opportunity to steal second.

"Newcombe didn't have that much of a curveball," Rivera said. "All of us knew that. But he had a good fastball. I was a fastball hitter, so it didn't bother me. Maybe he was irritated for hitting the ball right through the box. We always had the green light with the White Sox and when I was on first base I started swinging my arms back and forth like I was warming up to run. And Newcombe said, 'Look at him. He looks like he's in the jungle.'"

Rivera did try to steal second and Dodger catcher Roy Campanella threw him out, but the next day the remark was in the *Chicago Sun-Times* and the nickname stuck. Rivera didn't mind.

By 1953, Rivera was a regular in the White Sox outfield. He offered a mix of skills, hitting about a dozen home runs, driving in roughly 60 runs, and stealing about 20 bases a year. He was not a pure power hitter, but was dangerous at the plate. Nor was he a pure speedster, but took advantage of base-running chances. Rivera was one of the growing group of newcomers serving as building blocks for an aspiring White Sox team.

THE SETTING

Throughout the 1950s, the White Sox added talent, transforming the team from also-rans to pennant contenders. Billy Pierce joined up. Nellie Fox took over second base. Jim Landis roamed center field. Luis Aparicio came along. Jim Busby, Minnie Minoso, and Rivera himself might as well have been track stars, the way they sprinted around the bases.

"It started with Jim Busby," Rivera said of the Go-Go Sox theme. "Then we picked it up and everybody started hollering 'Go, go.' Our manager, Al Lopez, gave a lot of us the green light to go whenever we got on base unless the game was close. If we had a chance to steal, Luis and I, and Minnie and Jim Landis, were on our own."

When there were still only eight teams in each league and the majors had not yet expanded to the West Coast, road trips were shorter and teams traveled by train. Often they were overnight sleepers. The White Sox of the early 1950s played cards. The regular pinochle group included Rivera, Pierce, catcher Sherm Lollar, and pitcher Dick Donovan. They played for $5 a hand and Rivera remembers who dominated the standings.

"Not me!" he chuckled. "Lollar was the champ."

Although he never approached the single-season total again, Rivera's 16 triples in 1953 got plenty of attention. Triples are more rare than home runs and usually require a certain amount of daring.

"You check it out," Rivera said. "There are a lot of guys who don't really know how to run the bases. They're playing for home runs now. A lot of times a guy gets on base and looks at the coach all of the time instead of looking where the hell he's running. If you hit the ball in the right setting, before you ever get on the bases you know if a guy has a good arm and you have to be careful. In my era that was Roberto Clemente and Al Kaline. Those guys would not let you get that extra base. But if you hit it to right-center or right down the line and someone else was fielding, you knew you should be able to make a triple. And taking the extra base was the White Sox philosophy."

Up until 1959, Rivera said the biggest thrill he ever got from baseball was making his Major League debut with the Browns. That changed when the White Sox clinched the pennant.

THE GAME OF MY LIFE
BY JIM RIVERA

CHICAGO WHITE SOX VERSUS CLEVELAND INDIANS, SEPTEMBER 22, 1959

We knew we were going to win the pennant. It just felt like it was our turn. We didn't know what day we would clinch it, though, or how it would happen. We were hopeful when we went to Cleveland for that game. We had to beat them because they were the team behind us. The Indians were really hot and they had a great pitching staff. I felt we had to win.

We were ahead 2-0. Jim Perry started the game for the Indians, but Jim "Mudcat" Grant relieved him. The Indians had come back to within 2-1. In the sixth inning, Al Smith hit a solo home run and then I came up right after him and hit one. We ended up winning 4-2 and that was my biggest thrill. I was two-for-four that day.

We flew back to Chicago and, oh my goodness, it was wild. They had the horns blowing, bells ringing, and everything. It was quite a party.

GAME RESULTS

The victory over the Indians handed the White Sox a pennant for the first time in 40 years and propelled the team into the World Series against the Los Angeles Dodgers. The White Sox won the opener, 11-0, and felt pretty good about themselves. Then they ended up winning just one more game—a 1-0 masterpiece thrown by Bob Shaw, with a significant role played by Rivera—before losing the Series, 4-2, to L.A.

Manager Al Lopez juggled his lineup a little bit for Game 5's matchup at the Los Angeles Coliseum before 92,706 fans. The Dodgers were starting a then-little-known lefty named Sandy Koufax. Rivera was a lefty batter and Lopez chose to start right-handed hitter Jim McAnany. Late in the game, Lopez brought Rivera in as a defensive replacement in right field. Charlie Neal, the Dodgers' second baseman came up in the eighth inning and Rivera was familiar with his swing.

"I knew Charlie from playing with him in Puerto Rico and he hit a lot of balls to right-center," Rivera said. "I played him deep."

Sure enough, Neal got a hold of Shaw's offering early in the count and smoked it to right-center between Jim Landis and Rivera. Landis ran toward the fence, River retreated with a good jump, and as the ball came down, Rivera yelled, "I got it! I got it!" and caught it over his shoulder. It was an exciting moment for White Sox fans who briefly thought their club would come back against the Dodgers. But the Series ended one game later, just shy of the glory everyone in Chicago sought.

REFLECTIONS ON BASEBALL

Although he didn't know it at the time, Rivera's Major League career was winding down. He finished up in 1961 with the Kansas City Athletics.

Rivera's wife was from Angola, Indiana, about 100 miles from Chicago in a lake resort area, and after Rivera left baseball they settled there and opened a restaurant called the Captain's Cabin. They ran the restaurant for 26 years.

In 1976, during his second stint as owner of the White Sox, Bill Veeck borrowed Rivera for a day and turned him into a model. Veeck got the crazy idea that ballplayers might thrive during the hot summer months if they wore shorts. When Veeck introduced the Bermuda shorts outfit to the media, it was a bare-legged Rivera that showed off the threads. Joined by other ex-players Bill Skowron, Moe Drabowsky, Dave Nicholson, and Dan Osinski, Rivera arrived in a hotel lobby carrying a bat and declaring, "Love me!"

After a divorce, Rivera married again and moved to Fort Wayne, Indiana. In recent years, Rivera has kept in close contact with the White Sox, appearing at selected events. No event was more fun for Rivera than watching the 2005 Sox roll to the World Series title. Rivera, Pierce, Landis, Minoso, Aparicio, Shaw, and J.C. Martin attended the first two games at U.S. Cellular Field, posed for pictures with White Sox manager Ozzie Guillen, and were given the use of a sky box by owner Jerry Reinsdorf.

"That was fantastic," Rivera said.

CHAPTER 7

GARY PETERS

Gary Peters comes from a family of German-English descent. He attended Mercer High School in Pennsylvania and was such a star in basketball that he was named All-State. His achievements in baseball would come later, as the school did not field a team.

Peters' father, Tom, however, was a prominent figure in the sport in Western Pennsylvania. He had been a go-getter with talent noticed by both Pittsburgh and Cleveland when he was a young man. But he was married and the country was in the Depression when he came of age, so he was reluctant to give up a regular job for a chance at pro ball. Instead, Tom Peters played shortstop on the semi-pro circuit, traveling through the region for weekend games and sticking with the sport as an active player until he was 48. When Gary Peters was 12, he began taking trips with his old man to watch the games, and by the time he was 14 he was playing with him, sometimes holding down first base.

The elder Peters was showing signs of age and shifted to second base to shorten his throws as his arm weakened, but he kept playing as his son matured. From ages 14 to 18, Gary Peters played semi-pro ball with his dad and recalls that "it was a treat."

Occasionally Peters would pitch, but even when the White Sox took a look at him, scout Fred Shaffer pictured him as a first baseman/outfielder. Peters had a good day when Shaffer saw him.

"It worked out," Peters said. "I hit a ball out of the ballpark. I was just out of high school and it made me happy to sign. When I signed a deal with the White Sox, my dad made me play baseball as a summer job and go to college full-time at Grove City."

Grove City was not an NCAA school but Peters still competed on the school's basketball team. His first summer in the minors, in 1956, had Peters assigned to Holdredge in the Nebraska State League. It was a small town in a small league, yet when Peters arrived he was hardly the hottest prospect. The White Sox sent J.C. Martin to Nebraska, too, a player who had received a much larger bonus and eventually made it to the big club as a catcher.

At the time, Martin had first dibs on first base, Peters' usual position. Peters was shifted to right field. Several pitchers came down with sore arms and Peters demonstrated that he had a strong arm. The manager asked if he had any pitching experience and if he would like to give it a try.

"I won and I never got back off the mound," Peters said.

In 25 games, Peters compiled a 10-5 record with a 2.81 ERA. He led the league in strikeouts with 142 and was named the Nebraska State League's outstanding left-handed pitcher. As always, left-handed pitching was in demand, so the White Sox developed a strong interest in Peters' progress.

Peters' next stop was Dubuque in the Midwest League, where he replicated his season, going 10-6 with a 2.75 ERA. Over the next several seasons, the White Sox bounced Peters between Indianapolis and San Diego in AAA, interspersed with short stays in Chicago. Peters made his Major League debut with two appearances in 1959, but he was hardly a key factor in the pennant run. It wasn't until 1963 that Peters stuck with the parent club for good.

"I was winning 13, 12, 11 games in the minors, but you didn't just go up and get a start like you do now," he said. "They were end-of-season call-ups. It was getting a little bit frustrating. I was playing out my options, waiting to see if anybody else would pick me up. I wasn't pitching great, but I was winning."

For three straight years, Peters' White Sox record was 0-0, then 0-1. In all, he had a total of 20 Major League innings in the bank by 1962. Coming out of training camp in 1963, Peters was sure that he would be sent down to the minors again. But pitcher Juan Pizarro got sick with the flu and was going to miss his start. Pitching coach Ray Berres approached Peters on the team plane on the way to Kansas City and said, simply, "You're pitching."

Peters started, won the game, and even hit a home run. For once, Peters figured he had earned another start. But that wasn't the half of it: Peters emerged as the key man in the rotation, going 19-8 in a full season of play, with a league-leading ERA of 2.33. He won the rookie of the year award after at last getting a chance to prove himself.

Peters' dad was a passionate New York Yankees fan, and his son's call-up with the White Sox only partially turned him away from his lifelong rooting interest.

"The first big-league game I saw before I played—I think it was the only big-league game I saw, in the 1950s—was the Yankees at Cleveland," Peters said. "We were like 80 miles from Cleveland. My father went to a couple of World Series games with the Yankees back then. They got four guys together and went to New York. When I was in the majors with the White Sox, I used to ask him who he was rooting for when I was pitching against the Yankees. He said, 'I'm rooting for you tonight, but tomorrow night I'll be rooting for the Yankees.'"

THE SETTING

After years of yo-yoing between the big club and the minors, Peters exploded on the scene in 1963. He was an unheralded presence—a surprise for a team still trying to repeat its 1959 magic and seize another pennant. The White Sox shook up the team that season with a blockbuster trade that shipped reliever Hoyt Wilhelm and shortstop Luis Aparicio, both future Hall of Famers, to the Baltimore Orioles. Aparicio was so incensed that he declared the White Sox would not win a pennant again for 40 years. As it so happened, he turned out to be right.

Yet the White Sox came fairly close that season, finishing with a 94-68 record—second place, albeit 10½ games out. The White Sox hung in for a while, but the Yankees pulled away to win 104 games.

"Every game mattered," Peters mentioned about that season. And he remembers every game against the Yankees being magnified.

"They were tough," Peters said. "Somebody just sent me a score-card that I hadn't kept from that season. It was from a Yankees game where we beat them 2-0. My wife made me copies of them to sign. It was a Comiskey Park program that sold for 15 cents."

THE GAME OF MY LIFE
BY GARY PETERS

CHICAGO WHITE SOX VS. BALTIMORE ORIOLES, JULY 15, 1963

This was one of the best games I ever pitched. I threw a one-hitter at the Orioles and struck out 13 men without giving up a walk. I was in my first full year in the big leagues and Robin Roberts, the opposing pitcher, was nearing the end of his career. He was chosen for the Hall of Fame and won 286 games. Roberts had become famous with the Philadelphia Phillies, but he was still a dangerous pitcher with the Orioles (he won 14 games that year). Whenever you pitch a one-hitter, it seems like you've come close to a no-hitter. But Roberts got his hit, a single, early in the game (the third inning).

We touched him for four runs that day and while we didn't hit him hard, it was enough, the way I was pitching. But here's the funny thing about that game that keeps coming up. I play golf a lot in Florida with Robin Roberts and every time I see him he mentions the game because he got the only hit. He's always asking me, "Who's the best hitter you ever pitched to?"

I don't think about that game too much except Robby always brings it up. What he doesn't mention, and I don't remember it as well, is that I got two hits in the game. But he gave up 10 hits, so they didn't seem to matter as much.

This may have been the best game I ever pitched and I get reminded about it all of the time, not because it was such a good game, but because of the one "mistake." That's ironic.

GAME RESULTS

The White Sox won the game, 4-2, at Comiskey Park. The team was on its way to a second-place finish, the Orioles were on their way to a fourth-place finish, and Peters, whose record was just 7-5 after the win, was on his way to a terrific 12-3 stretch to finish the year. At one point he won 11 games in a row.

"There were no playoffs in those days," Peters said of the Division Series and League Championship Series. "It was just the World Series. If you got beat by a game or two you'd think back and wonder where you lost it."

Peters hurled 243 innings in 1963, not an inordinate amount, though one that would lead the American League these days. He also threw 13 complete games, completely unheard of today.

One of Peters' specialty pitches was a sinker. Batters swung away and stroked a lot of ground balls. That meant Peters didn't have to go deep into the count all of the time.

"I had a lot of low-pitch games," Peters said, "but we also had games where we would throw 130 pitches. Juan Pizarro pitched a complete game in Chicago one year and somebody who kept the charts said he threw 160-some pitches. He was throwing as good in the ninth as he was throwing in the first."

If a pitching coach or manager allowed a starter to throw 160 pitches in 2008 he would probably be fired.

"Oh, god, yeah," Peters said. "In my day we had Hoyt Wilhelm as a reliever. We didn't have a short man and a long man. A few years ago a lot of us were in Chicago for the White Sox team-of-the-century announcement. Wilbur Wood was there and so was Frank Thomas."

Wood once threw 376⅔ innings in a season and started both games of a doubleheader. When Thomas heard that about the 1970s performance, he shook his head.

"Frank looked at me and said, 'Is that true?' I said, 'Sure it's true.' Frank couldn't believe it."

REFLECTING ON BASEBALL

Gary Peters pitched a second one-hitter for the White Sox on May 14, 1967, besting the California Angels, 3-1. He surrendered a run, though, so it wasn't quite the gem his first one was. The southpaw stayed with the White Sox through the 1969 season, then played his final three years with the Boston Red Sox. Included in that late-career run was a 16-11 mark with Boston in 1970.

The White Sox parted with Peters after a groin injury ruined his 1968 season, and they wondered if he would ever be the same again. Peters pulled his groin in May, and when he tried to keep pitching he aggravated his problems by overcompensating, ending up with a sore elbow. He said the pain persisted until December, after the season. Peters won 10 games the next year, but then went to Boston.

Peters attended college at Grove City in his home town in Pennsylvania as he began his minor league career. When he finished his Major League career, he settled in Sarasota, Florida, and took some courses at Manatee College focusing on building construction. He spent 15 years working for a private contractor, often building enormous supermarkets. Then, after tiring of the travel, he hooked up with his local school board, administering the construction of new schools in the district.

In retirement, Peters is an active golfer who participates in charity events. Once a year the old White Sox get together and play in a charity golf tournament. He doesn't follow baseball as closely as he once did, with a few exceptions. If a pitcher he admires is on TV, particularly Greg Maddux, Tom Glavine, or Randy Johnson, Peters settles into a comfortable seat to watch.

And if the White Sox are on television in Sarasota, Peters will try to watch his old team.

CHAPTER 8

JOEL HORLEN

Baseball was big in Joel Horlen's family when he was growing up in San Antonio, Texas. His father, Kermit, played in what Horlen described as "the Sunday beer league," and his younger brother Bill was an avid player. Horlen's first baseball affiliation was with the local YMCA. His father coached the team and one of his playmates was Gary Bell, also a future Major League pitcher. Horlen went on to the Pony League and competed in American Legion ball after that. Horlen said he had scouts looking at him, but his parents had other ideas of what he should be doing at age 17.

"My mom and dad wanted me to go to college if I could find a scholarship somewhere," he said.

The summer before he enrolled in Oklahoma State, Horlen was signed by a semi-pro team out of Alpine, Texas. Under NCAA rules he could make no more than $350 for his summer job, but that job entailed roaming through Texas, Oklahoma, and Arizona for a 65-game schedule that sent Horlen to the mound 16 times. The exposure and the experience proved very helpful during Horlen's three years at Oklahoma State, where he was selected as an All-American and the school won the 1959 College World Series.

"I probably got the best tip of my life while I was out there (on the summer circuit)," Horlen recalled. "There was a scout for the Red Sox and he gave me the best tip on how to grab, how to hold a fastball when I was pitching. I was holding the ball with my fingers spread and the ball came in pretty straight. He showed me a grip and said, 'You start throwing this and your control might not be too good for a week or two, but if you stick with it, it's gonna help you more than anything you've ever done before.' He was absolutely right."

Horlen struggled at first in the minors. He found himself playing for San Diego in the Pacific Coast League in 1961 and again it was good advice from a seasoned pro that helped the youngster. Herb Score, who was a dazzling flamethrower of the 1950s for the Indians before being injured, was sent to San Diego to regain his form.

"Herb Score came down and he took me under his wing and really made me work hard between starts, running, and a lot of stuff like that, and I think my physical strength became more dominant and enabled me to be more successful and stay on the mound for nine innings," Horlen reflected in a 1995 interview.

Horlen broke in with the White Sox in a minimal role in 1961, but by 1963 he was a full-fledged member of the starting rotation. He also fell under the spell of Chicago's legendary pitching coach, Ray Berres.

"I learned a lot about how to share knowledge with other players from Ray Berres," Horlen said. "Ray Berres' psychology was that if you don't have good mechanics, you're not gonna have good stuff. That's about all we talked about when I was in Chicago—mechanics. Fortunately, I picked up a lot of what he was saying. I had a couple of bad habits when I got there and he fixed them up."

THE SETTING

Joel Horlen won 11 games for the White Sox in 1963 and he hovered in the 10-13 win range for a few seasons before enjoying a breakout won-loss year in 1967. Horlen had shown his potential in '63, though, when his 1.88 ERA was second best in the league. When Horlen began bargaining for a new contract, the White Sox brought up the point that he was only four games over .500 at 11-7 and never mentioned the ERA. A mild-mannered player, Horlen was determined to get what he thought he was worth, and he was making less than $14,000 a year.

"They try to get you as cheap as they can," he said during negotiations. "You try to get more than you're probably worth."

This comment, reported in *The Sporting News* in early 1965, was likely as accurate and as succinct an observation ever made about athlete-team contract negotiations.

During the 1967 season it became known that Horlen experimented with all types of substances in order to avoid dry mouth while pitching. He tried chewing tobacco, but it made him ill. He tried bubble gum, but didn't stick with it. He even tried chewing adhesive tape to keep his saliva juiced up during a game, but the "gummy substance comes off the cloth and you've got nothing to clamp your teeth on." So Horlen began chewing on tissues. He scrunched them up, placed a little bit between his teeth and gums, and chomped on them as he pitched.

Apparently this worked, because Horlen had a great season that year. He threw six shutouts and the White Sox were immersed in one of the greatest pennant races of all time. In the end, the Sox finished fourth, just three games out of first in the Boston Red Sox's Impossible Dream season. The performance was so named because the Red Sox leapt from ninth to first in the then-10-team American League in one season to reach the World Series.

With a week to go in the regular season, however, the Red Sox, White Sox, Detroit Tigers, and Minnesota Twins all had a shot at the title. When Horlen went to the mound for his regular turn in mid-September to face the Tigers at Comiskey Park in the opening game of a doubleheader, the White Sox were still very much alive.

THE GAME OF MY LIFE
BY JOEL HORLEN

CHICAGO WHITE SOX VS. DETROIT TIGERS, SEPTEMBER 10, 1967

The day I pitched my no-hitter we had lost a heartbreaker of a game the night before. I tried never to let things like that bother me. I just knew what my job was and how to go about it. I had good stuff that season, my best. I held the ball one way and it sank, but if I held it another way it would cut the other way. I had two types of curveballs and I had a real big, sweeping curve for strikeouts. I used a smaller breaking curve when I was behind in the count. Many thanks to Whitey Ford for that.

One day, Tommy John and I were talking to Ford in New York. Tommy wasn't afraid to ask anything. Whitey (a future Hall of Famer) could throw his curveball at 3-0 and make it break for a strike any time he wanted to do so. Tommy asked him how he did it. He showed us his grip. It was a little unorthodox. We both tried it and we both used it. It was really helpful. For a while, when I was playing a lot of charity golf tournaments, I would be asked, "What was that thing you threw? It was a little short curveball thing." I'd say, "That's my secret weapon."

I wouldn't even tell hitters after I retired. I still hated them. Let them worry about it at night. On the day I started against the Tigers we were close to the front in the standings and we were definitely thinking pennant. Every game was very important. It was September and we were really trying to make up any ground we could.

Baseball players are superstitious, and that year I went to some function the day before the season started. I made an appearance where I had to wear a coat and tie. Not my favorite thing. But I wore a coat and tie to the ballpark. I pitched well and won. So I thought, "Maybe there's something to it." So I did it the rest of the year. We had to wear them on the road anyway, but on the days I pitched, I wore a coat and tie, even at home games.

I knew it was a big game. I felt more tired than usual, but hell, you always feel a little off. I just wanted to get that first pitch over with. After that first pitch, it was just another game. It helped that we scored five runs in the first inning.

I had been pitching well and I didn't have to worry about my command. I just took it for granted that I was going to have it. I just tried to keep the ball low. Joe Sparma started for the Tigers, but he didn't get out of the first inning. The Tigers were on their third pitcher, Dave Wickersham, when I came up in the third inning. I got hit by a pitch. I had hit their catcher, Bill Freehan, who was a friend of mine, but they didn't think it was an accident. He had been hit the last two games in a row and first time up I hit him. Oh, he was mad. I said, "Bill, are you all right?" He called me all kinds of names.

When I came up, the first pitch was right at my head. I kind of knew it was coming, so I got out of the way. I thought maybe he (Wickersham) was just letting me know he didn't appreciate things. That was fine with me. The second pitch was at my ribs and how I got out of the way I don't know. I wasn't looking for it, but I thought, "Well, that's it. That's gonna be it." And the next one's at my legs. I got my left leg out of the way, but the ball hit me on the inside of my right knee. It was like somebody hit me with an ironing board. I went down and then got up and limped over to first base. They wanted to take me out of the game, but I didn't want to go. I had things going good. From that inning on I was afraid to sit down because I would stiffen up. For the rest of the game, when I wasn't on the mound, I walked around the dugout and into the tunnel to the clubhouse.

The leg never really did stiffen up until after the game when I got home. I'd completely forgotten about it before the game was over. About the sixth inning I became conscious of the fact that I hadn't given up a hit. There were some really good hitters in the Tigers' line-up. Freehan, Al Kaline, Willie Horton, Dick McAuliffe.

McAuliffe made the last out in the ninth inning. He hit a grounder to Ron Hansen at shortstop and I saw the throw. I saw it was going to be good. Cotton Nash was at first base and caught it. He had come in for defensive purposes. When the umpire called the runner out I remember throwing my glove up and everybody hopping up and down.

I didn't act too excited with the reporters afterward. I don't think I was ever a real good interview. I didn't have anything earth shattering to tell anybody. It was just a game that we needed to win and they didn't get any hits.

GAME RESULTS

The White Sox won, 6-0, then swept the doubleheader on a combined five-hitter by rookie starter Francisco Carlos, Hoyt Wilhelm, and Bob Locker, to tighten up the pennant race.

The postgame noise in the locker room made up for the late-game silence in the dugout. Observing time-honored tradition, Horlen's teammates had refused to talk to him in the late innings, lest they jinx the no-hitter. It seemed as if the Comiskey fans abided by the same protocol.

"I was thinking about it all right," Horlen said afterward. "It was real quiet in the dugout. Even the fans were quiet. Anyway, I didn't hear a thing."

Detroit put one runner on base on an error and had a second runner—Freehan—because of Horlen's plunking. He walked no one and struck out four in his nine innings. The best White Sox catch in the game was of a hard-hit line drive off Kaline's bat in the fourth inning. Second baseman Wayne Causey speared it. With his fast sinker working smoothly, Horlen induced 18 ground-ball outs.

After the victory, a game ball was sent to the National Baseball Hall of Fame in Cooperstown, New York, but Horlen kept a souvenir of the occasion too.

"I've got the ball from the last out," he said.

REFLECTING ON BASEBALL

Horlen had come close to a no-hitter one time before that game. Throwing against the Washington Senators on July 29, 1963, he took a no-hitter into the ninth inning before only 4,769 fans in D.C.

"There was an umpire behind the plate and I won't name him, but he had a horrendous reputation for a very small strike zone," Horlen said. "I'm going out for the seventh inning and I haven't given up a hit yet. On the way out he comes down to me—I've already walked four or five guys and I never walk that many in a game—and I've got a 1-0 lead. He says, 'Get it close and I'll help you out. I've never umpired a no-hitter.'

"Everybody hated pitching when he was behind the plate. I started to tell him, 'With that strike zone you've got, you never will.' But I bit my tongue and didn't say anything. I got to the ninth inning. Chuck Hinton came to the plate and he hits a ground ball that I just barely miss. Ron Hansen was playing short and he barely missed it. That was the first hit. Now I've got a 1-0 lead."

The no-hitter was gone, but the ballgame was at issue.

"Bobo Osborne, a big, left-handed hitter, comes up," Horlen said. "I get to 3-2 on him and we're so close. Osborne hits the perfect double-play ball and we can only throw to first base. The next guy up was Don Lock. He could hit home runs."

Only a short while earlier, Horlen had faced Lock in Chicago and struck him out twice in four at-bats by throwing a curveball.

"I lobbed him a curveball up and he hits it for a home run," Horlen said. "We got beat 2-1. As soon as he hit the ball, I knew it was gone. It really was a disappointment."

After Horlen retired, he carved out a successful career in private business. In the late 1980s, Horlen was invited to a White Sox reunion and he came into the city early with his wife, Lois, to visit old friends. She had never been to New York City, so they extended their trip.

When they checked into their hotel, Horlen noticed that the Mets were playing a home game. The Mets manager was Davey Johnson, also from San Antonio, and a good friend of Horlen's. Horlen called Johnson and left a message. Johnson called back and told Horlen he was going to leave tickets at the will call window. When Horlen and Lois reached the park, they were greeted by Mets officials, taken to the Shea Stadium owner's box, and wooed with a job offer to join the club's minor-league system. The team had called periodically, but Horlen was not interested in a career change—until then.

In 1987, he joined the Mets and began coaching in spring training, then did a minor league tour. Eventually, he moved to the Giants' organization and was the pitching coach at AAA Phoenix for five years. Horlen earned a rep as a troubleshooter who corrected deliveries—the old mechanics lessons from Berres were still valuable.

"They called me 'The Fixer,'" Horlen said of how the Giants used him with young pitchers. "Russ Ortiz was probably the most prominent player I helped. He was 2-6 in Shreveport in AA and they sent him to me. It took me about 30 seconds to spot his problem. He went 6-2 and went to the big leagues."

Horlen retired from baseball a second time in 2001, but he will always keep track of the White Sox' fortunes from a distance.

CHAPTER 9

BOB SHAW

Bob Shaw was a city kid from the Bronx, but he experienced his earliest moments in organized play while living in Garden City, Long Island. Shaw's father, John, was a tremendous athlete, playing basketball and football, as well as racing on the swim and track teams in high school. He later coached football and became director of physical education in Garden City after earning degrees at New York University. The young Shaw, born in 1933, had advanced to American Legion play in his teens, but was then shipped off to a northern New England prep school, Kimball Union Academy in Meriden, New Hampshire, and honed his skills there. Shaw was an all-around athlete, but at that point in his life his career goal was to become a doctor. He wanted to enroll in Dartmouth, but there was one problem.

"I didn't have the grades," he said.

Instead, Shaw enrolled at St. Lawrence University in northern New York where he was majoring in pre-med. Shaw attended classes for two and a half years, but then decided he wasn't going to spend his career carrying a little black bag around making house calls. He transferred to Adelphi College, back on Long Island, and changed his major to physical education. Although Shaw spent three semesters at Adelphia he was advancing his baseball education at least as swiftly.

While pitching for St. Lawrence, he was noticed and invited to a try-out camp.

"I went and I ended up trying out for seven or eight teams," Shaw said.

The Tigers' Ray Garland liked Shaw the most. But when nothing immediately came of the tryout he went back to St. Lawrence and played football. He was the quarterback and starting safety on the gridiron.

"Football was probably my favorite and I just said sure when they asked me to try out," Shaw said. "I had no idea that I'd play professional baseball. Not the slightest."

However, the tryout led to a contract offer from the Tigers and when school ended, Shaw joined the Detroit organization and was sent to Jamestown in the New York-Penn League to play rookie ball. Gradually, Shaw, the accidental pro pitcher, worked his way through the Detroit minor-league system—Durham, North Carolina, Augusta, Georgia, Syracuse, Toronto, and Charleston, South Carolina—and reached the big club in 1957 for seven appearances. But in the spring of 1958, when the Tigers farmed him out again, he went on strike instead of throwing strikes. He staged a 12-day walk-out, refusing to report.

Shaw had also spent off-seasons pitching in Cuba, and things sometimes got a little bit testy around the old ballpark. Machine guns were as common as bats, and once, when he heard a round being chambered in a rifle not far from him, he ran off the mound. Still, the real reason Shaw walked out on the Tigers was his belief in his own abilities, that he could play at the highest level of the game.

"I knew I could pitch in the big leagues," Shaw told *Sports Illustrated* after he burned up the American League in 1959. "All I wanted was a chance."

The rebellion resulted in change on June 15 when Shaw was traded to the White Sox in a deal featuring Ray Boone and Tito Francona. Shaw finished 4-2 and played in 29 games, but it turned out to be only the vamp. Shaw saw minimal action during his first two seasons in the big leagues, but he exploded on the American League scene in

1959 with his unexpected 18-6 record. Sox manager Al Lopez and pitching coach Ray Berres saw beyond Shaw's inexperience and worked closely with him. Previously, Shaw varied his delivery, throwing side-arm to right-handed batters and overhand to left-handed swingers. He started throwing overhand to all hitters.

"To get there with Berres and Lopez, that was a break for me," Shaw said.

THE SETTING

Shaw was just what the White Sox needed—another good, strong arm to take a spot in the rotation. It was early in the season when Shaw projected himself into White Sox lore in one of the strangest games the team ever played.

On April 22, 1959, Early Wynn started the game against the Kansas City Athletics. In an otherwise spectacular season (during which he won the Cy Young Award), Wynn had nothing that day. He was pummelled for six runs in 1⅔ innings. Shaw was brought into the game in the second inning and went the rest of the way, hurling 7⅓ innings. In a season when victories would be plentiful for the right-hander, Shaw's record was 1-0 at the end of the day.

What distinguished the game played at Municipal Stadium in Kansas City from so many others was not only the final score of 20-6, but how the White Sox scored. In a double-figure-run seventh inning, the Sox stunned their opponents and all 7,446 witnesses in the stands, by scoring 11 runs on one hit. They also collected 10 walks and a hit batsmen in the inning. The White Sox accumulated 16 hits on the day, with second baseman Nellie Fox collecting four of them.

"I still have some people come up and ask, 'Do you remember?' about that game," Shaw said nearly 40 years later. "That was really something. My goodness, it was incredible."

Such a game might have been a portent for the Sox, that good fortune would be with them, that being the Go-Go White Sox with patience at the plate and daring on the basepaths would pay off. The

White Sox won 94 games and Shaw did his share in the most productive season of his career.

The White Sox played the World Series well against the Dodgers, but by the time Shaw was handed the ball by Lopez to start the fifth game, the team trailed 3-1. The Dodgers needed only one more win to wrap it up. So Shaw was the designated savior for the White Sox.

A Series record crowd of 92,706 fans paid its way into the Los Angeles Coliseum that day. The starting pitcher for the Dodgers was a comparatively unheralded left-hander by the name of Sandy Koufax. No one could foresee that future Hall of Famer Koufax was about to break out as the best pitcher in the National League.

THE GAME OF MY LIFE
BY BOB SHAW

CHICAGO WHITE SOX VS. LOS ANGELES DODGERS, WORLD SERIES GAME 5, OCTOBER 6, 1959

I knew I was going to start the fifth game. I started the second game, but we lost 4-3 and I gave up all four runs. I knew I was going to pitch again.

They were all afternoon World Series games at the time, so you got up, ate breakfast and went to the ballpark. You didn't really eat a lot before the game. I remember my parents were coming, family members, having to set them up in a hotel, book flights—it was very hectic. Then, of course, there was the media. With the media attention, there were people, this, that, and the other thing. To be honest, it was almost as if it were a break to go pitch in the ballgame.

I always felt the pressure in any game because you didn't want to let the team or the fans down or embarrass your family. So you just wanted to do a good job and you wanted to win. That's the kind of pressure you inflicted on yourself. You don't know that it's the largest crowd in the history of the World Series, but you know there's a lot of people. You also know there's television and there could be 10, 15, or 20 million people watching.

It was a game that if you didn't have it, you knew the World Series was over. By winning that game at least it brought the Series back to Chicago. I'm sure the owners were happy about that because they made a little more money. You knew the pressure was on. You just had to concentrate on what you had to do. Some people handle it better than others, to be honest with you.

We got one run in the fourth inning to take the lead and that was the only run in the ballgame. It was a pretty short left-field wall, at 250 feet. I remember all of the people sitting out there in centerfield with white shirts making it hard to see the ball when Koufax threw. It helped me, too, but it was very hard to see Koufax. The guy was exceptional. He had great stuff, a great fastball, a great curveball. A lot of people didn't know that he had a great curveball, but he was a notch above everybody. So if you beat him you had to be a little on the lucky side.

I pitched 7⅓ innings and then we brought in Billy Pierce and Dick Donovan, and finally we won and sent the Series back to Chicago. I'm not a big sports memorabilia collector, but I do have some different balls from different seasons—I believe I have a ball from that Series.

GAME RESULTS

The White Sox won 1-0. The only run was scored on a Dodger double play that Sox catcher Sherm Lollar hit into. Nellie Fox, who was on third base, scored. At the time it was logical for the Dodgers to take two outs and surrender the run. The big surprise was that no one scored again. Shaw gave up nine hits with one walk and one strikeout. Four of them came off the bat of Jim Gilliam and three were stroked by Gil Hodges. Koufax gave up only five hits with six strikeouts.

The victory brought the World Series back to Comiskey Park for a Game 6, but LA polished off the Sox, 9-3, ending the team's 1959 run. Although they fell short of the ultimate prize, White Sox fans and the organization were very happy with the pennant and felt the team was ready for a long stretch at the top.

Just before the season, colorful Bill Veeck became owner of the team and he was excited about the prospect of capturing several pennants. However, in some of the worst decisions he made as a four-time, three-team owner, Veeck traded away several future stars for players he thought could pay instant dividends in the 1960 pennant race. Such players as Earl Battey, Johnny Romano, and Norm Cash departed and their replacements were not as valuable. The Sox "dynasty" died after a single pennant.

In the off-season, Shaw worked out doubly hard, conditioning by doing push-ups and pull-ups, swimming, running, and playing handball and badminton. Shaw was a stickler for a healthy routine during the season, as well.

"I like to work extra hard in preparing for a game," Shaw said at the time. "When you know you're a starter you can get the proper rest two nights before the game. You can eat your meals properly. You can get yourself mentally and physically alert."

Yet none of that effort helped in 1960 when Shaw finished 13-13 with an ERA of 4.06 instead of the preceding season's 2.69, and although he had success in other venues, Shaw never had another White Sox season to match 1959.

REFLECTING ON BASEBALL

Shaw spent two full years and part of a third in the White Sox rotation before being shipped to Kansas City. Just as he did in Detroit when he felt he was being treated unfairly, Shaw protested when the White Sox wanted to slash his salary.

"If the Chicago White Sox don't want me, I don't want the Chicago White Sox," he said during spring training in 1961. "I've yielded as much as I intend to. I'm ready to be traded."

The White Sox obliged him, but in 1962 Shaw emerged once again as a devastating starting pitcher for the Milwaukee Braves. He went 15-9 in 38 games and notched a 2.80 earned run average. But things soured quickly. About a week or so later, pitching against the Philadelphia Phillies, Shaw popped and tore a tendon in his throwing shoulder. Shaw went through rehab, but his arm strength was slow to return and he became a relief pitcher for the Braves. He had one more big-time season left in the arm after moving on to the Giants. In 1965, Shaw finished 16-9 with a 2.64 ERA.

"Frank Lary tore the same tendon and never came back," Shaw said of a top starter of that time period. "Vernon Law took two years to come back. We all popped it the same year and I came back the next, but I ended up in short relief. I could warm up, but there was less strain if I pitched an inning or two, whereas as a starter you have to go seven, eight, nine innings."

After returning to Jupiter, Florida, full time, Shaw worked in commercial real estate—he still has an office—developing shopping malls and office buildings. He says he has been a lucky man. Shaw saved only a small percentage of memorabilia. He said his long-time wife Asta got a bit upset when she discovered that things he parted with had become valuable. Shaw also joked to a sports collectors magazine upon learning that one of his cards was valued at $75, "I didn't know I was worth that much. Probably for a nickel or a dime my wife would give me away."

Given the time that has passed since he was a member of the White Sox, and given how rarely Shaw gets the opportunity to mingle with ex-teammates, he says the Sox are still No. 1 in his heart.

"My second team would be the Braves because I pitched in the All-Star game for them," Shaw said, "and I had a couple of good years with them. But I would say that I root for the White Sox more than anybody. The 1959 World Series game when I beat Koufax was my biggest thrill in baseball."

CHAPTER 10

J.C. MARTIN

Joseph Clifton Martin grew up in the small town of Martinsville, Virginia, although his family lived on the outskirts, about 10 miles from downtown. That location inhibited Martin's early involvement in organized sports.

"It was very difficult for me to get to town," he said, "so I didn't play but one year. They called it Junior Commerce baseball."

When he reached high school, Martin became a more active baseball player, competing on local semi-pro teams with older men, and the seasoning against them paid off when Martin was noticed by scouts. Martin was a first baseman and third baseman, but he didn't carry a big stick—he never would—and it was determined that if he was going to stay in the big leagues he would have to become a catcher. Good fielding catchers who gain the confidence of the pitching staff are at a premium.

Martin played in three games for the 1959 White Sox pennant winners and saw minimal action in 1960. He got into 110 games in 1961, but batted only .230. In the next season he made 18 appearances for the White Sox, but by then his future was being guided by higher-ups on the club.

"They changed me all around and gave me a great big raise to go to the minor leagues to catch," Martin said, that so-called big-time payoff being only $1,000. "That was like great big money," Martin laughed.

When Martin was asked to become a catcher, the White Sox were thin at the position throughout the organization. This was a byproduct of Bill Veeck's ill-fated trades of Earl Battey and Johnny Romano, both of whom enjoyed very productive Major League careers elsewhere.

"That hurt the White Sox for about 10 years," Martin said.

Martin wasn't sure who made the decision to ship him out, but Sox manager Al Lopez, a Hall of Fame catcher himself, gave him the news. Lopez promised to bring him back as a first baseman-third baseman if "you cannot do it." The White Sox gave Martin his money and farmed him out to Savannah in the South Atlantic, or Sally League, to gain instruction under manager Les Moss, a former catcher.

"It was quite a challenge," Martin said, who weighed the extra money and the promise of a return to the big club roster in accepting. "I had a young family and we weren't making any money. So I said OK."

Not only was Martin taught by Moss, but when the regular season ended he followed Moss to Venezuela for winter ball to cram in more experience.

"J.C. was green at the start," Moss said a year after tutoring Martin, "but he took to the job naturally. You could see him improving from week to week and by the end of the winter league I was sure he could catch in the big leagues. And what an arm. Nobody stole on him."

Moss was complimentary, but Martin said becoming a catcher was tough.

"When you go back there (behind the plate) and you've got all the equipment on and stuff, you have to learn to ignore it," he said. "Balls are hitting in the dirt and you have to always keep your eyes open. You cannot flinch. When the ball comes in and the guy swings the bat, if you flinch, you don't know where the ball goes.

"It was my job to set the hitter up and make the pitcher comfortable so that he just concentrates on spots. I work on the hitter's weakness. It turned out really well. A little while ago I got a call from

Chicago and they said I'm the only catcher who has caught more than 4,000 innings whose pitchers had an ERA under 3.00. I thought that was a pretty good thing to hear."

Martin also learned first-hand about those aches and pains that catchers endure that cut seasons off of their careers.

"You have to learn to play injured," Martin said. "In Savannah, I had a broken finger, a compound dislocation. The bone came through the skin. Les Moss put it back and then he took one of those soft ice trays that you put in the freezer and bent the tray holder and taped it around my finger."

Martin played in the Sally League with up-and-comers like Don Buford and Dave DeBusschere, who gained more fame as a basketball player for the New York Knicks than as a short-time pitcher with the Sox. DeBusschere was a top-notch starter on the Savannah team, according to Martin, but was trying to pursue both sports professionally and the White Sox wanted him to give up hoops.

Catcher is probably the most difficult position to play, and for Martin it was like learning a foreign language. His challenge was compounded by the fact that the White Sox featured tough-to-catch knuckleballers like Hoyt Wilhelm and Eddie Fisher.

Martin became a catcher immediately after the Baltimore Orioles outfitted catcher Gus Triandos with an oversized mitt in order for him to cope with Wilhelm. The glove was jokingly called the "pillow" mitt because it was so large. The circumference was measured at 41 inches. However, the Major League rules committee slapped a maximum size of 38 inches on catchers mitts. No one was impacted more than the White Sox and Martin. The team pooled brainpower with Wilson Sporting Goods to invent a new mitt meeting specifications that was supposed to grip better. Martin still sounded like he was pining for the giant glove at the beginning of the 1965 season.

"I believe you need all the leather you can get back there in order to block that pitch," he said. "I'd like to have all the glove I can handle."

By the end of that season, renowned Chicago baseball writer Jerome Holtzman wrote that Martin deserved "a baseball purple heart with clusters" for handling Wilhelm's and Fisher's crazy stuff. New glove or not, Martin had more than 30 passed balls. Martin's catching limitations were not blamed—the pitchers' pitch was.

THE SETTING

By 1967, it was clear that Martin had made the right choice in adapting to catcher. He fielded well and called a good game, though he was never a significant threat at the plate. Wilhelm, who had a storied caree—setting records for appearances and establishing the role of reliever as a respectable career choice—was the first relief pitcher elected to the Hall of Fame. He was unflappable—no doubt a useful trait for a knuckleballer—and despite Martin's frequent battles keeping those pitches in play, he raved about the catcher's skills.

"J.C.'s the best that's ever caught me," Wilhelm said in the 1960s. "He's strong and he's quick. I've had some good catchers before, but he's the best."

It is ironic, though perhaps not surprising, that regardless of all of the attention he received for catching-related activities, just about Martin's favorite moment in a Majo League game occurred in the batter's box. During the 1967 season four teams were in the American League pennant race into the final week. Anyone who had a hand in a victory knew it was important for the team. Martin, who hit just 32 homers in his entire big-league career, relishes one of them above all, particularly because it was a game-winner.

That summer, the White Sox had some extraordinary contests with the Cleveland Indians, a team that was out of the mix fighting for the pennant. Once, the teams played 16 innings. During another series they played 17. While the Indians were not as strong as the front-runners, they had some pitchers who could do damage. In a late-July encounter, the Sox faced southpaw Sam McDowell. Nicknamed "Sudden" because of the speed of his fastball, McDowell struck Bob Gibson-like fear into batters.

McDowell was on the mound for the Indians, not at his absolute finest, but throwing very well. Martin was sent into the game as a defensive replacement for Jerry McNertney in the eighth inning, but had not yet batted.

THE GAME OF MY LIFE
BY J.C. MARTIN

CHICAGO WHITE SOX VS. CLEVELAND INDIANS, JULY 25, 1967

I don't know what it was, but we always had tough games against Cleveland. We sort of managed to beat them most of the time somehow, but they always played us tough.

We were in another of those tough games against the Indians with Sam McDowell pitching and it was in the same series where we played them 16 innings. It was in the ninth inning and I always had really good success against Cleveland pitchers. I didn't hit against McDowell much because he was a left-hander. I platooned a lot and I hit against the right handers. There was one period in the mid-1960s where the Indians had four left-handed starters.

I remember one time when we were playing the Indians, Pete Ward, our third baseman, showed up at the ballpark and said, "Man, I'm telling you, I had a rough night." I asked why. He said, "I dreamed one of those left-handers was throwing and he pitched me inside and I fell out of bed." Pete was a left-handed hitter and he dreamed he had faced four straight starters, all left-handed. Good gosh, that's a nightmare.

In the game against McDowell, our manager, Eddie Stanky, had used up all of his right-handed pinch-hitters by the ninth inning so he left me in the game. Then someone got on first base. It was 1-1. I came up to bat and hit a home run off him and we won the game.

They had a good pitching staff and a good ballclub, but we just managed to come out on top most of the time.

GAME RESULTS

When J.C. Martin came to the plate in the ninth it was a tie game. Tommie Agee, who had walked, was on first base. There was one out. Martin's walk-off homer provided the final score of 3-1— White Sox win. Sam McDowell, who had pitched 8⅓ innings of fine baseball, absorbed the loss; he permitted three runs on six hits, while striking out six.

In the big picture, it was just a regular-season game that the White Sox needed in the pennant race, though they finished three games out. For Martin personally, it lingered as a special occasion. One reason his memory of the homer is so clear is that the brief encounter between Martin and McDowell did not end there. During a 1968 spring training exhibition game in Tucson, Arizona, Martin came to the plate again against McDowell. Seven months had passed since the home run. Martin stepped into the batter's box and McDowell unleashed a fastball.

"The first pitch hit me right in the ribs," Martin said. "Joe Azcue was catching for Cleveland and he reached over, picked up the ball, and said, 'Long memory, huh, Jay?'"

Martin can laugh about the bruised ribs decades later, as he's always been a forgiving guy. Very religious, Martin printed brochures of his testimony that he passed out at events where he was asked to speak. The cover of the brochure featured a picture of Martin wearing catcher's gear and in block print said, "Converted Catcher, Chicago Cubs."

Martin ended up playing the last three years of his career for the Cubs.

"I had been raised in the church," he wrote. "Mother taught Sunday school and my younger brother Melvin and I were there almost every time the doors opened. The preacher got close to me. Although I didn't drink, smoke, or swear, I realized the need of trusting in Christ as my Saviour. I did and have been trying to follow Him ever since. No telling where I would be today if I had not started my baseball career as a Christian."

Martin was surprised to learn that a copy of his testimony brochure was in his player file at the National Baseball Hall of Fame library.

REFLECTIONS ON BASEBALL

Martin retired in 1972, but coached for the Cubs organization the next two years before entering private business, first with a rubber company, then with a residential home building company, and then with Prestige Nursery, near Wheaton, Illinois. Around 1995, Martin moved to Advance, North Carolina, a small town near Winston-Salem and only 60 miles from his old home in Virginia. He watches the minor-league team in Winston-Salem, but spends considerable time golfing. Besides watching the nearby minor leaguers, Martin makes pilgrimages to the Chicago area to watch his grandson pitch. He has two daughters in North Carolina and a son who still lives in Wheaton and is the Wheaton College golf coach.

Once in a while Martin has a banquet rendezvous with former White Sox teammates like Luis Aparicio, Jim Landis, Bob Shaw, and Pete Ward. He saw a lot of the old gang in Chicago at the 2005 World Series.

Sometimes they overlap at charity events. If someone throws a golf tournament and one-time teammates are going, Martin's there. And if he ever runs into Sam McDowell, he may just plunk him in the ribs with a drive off the first tee.

CHAPTER 11

PETE WARD

Pete Ward was born in Montreal in 1939, where his father, Jimmy, was a professional hockey player skating on wing for the old Montreal Maroons and the Canadiens as part of a 13-year National Hockey League career.

Ward was eight years old when his father retired and the family moved to Portland, Oregon. Until then, Ward's favorite sport had been hockey. Sportswriters during Ward's early days with the White Sox hinted that he could have become a two-sport professional, but Ward said he had barely begun to play before the Wards relocated to Oregon. A regular attendee at Blackhawks games during the Bobby Hull-Stan Mikita era when he lived in Chicago, Ward still loves to watch the game, though he doesn't follow it with the same intensity since the NHL expanded from six teams to 30.

"It's funny now because there are so many teams you can throw the nicknames at me and I can't tell you what city they're from," Ward said.

Growing up in Portland in the 1950s, Ward was far removed from Major League baseball. To him, the apex of the baseball world meant the local Portland Beavers minor league team.

"I didn't know that much about the Major Leagues," Ward said. "All I knew about Chicago was that it was in the middle of the country."

Ward started playing baseball in Oregon, including a stint on a local team called "The Mecca Lunch." Ward's baseball horizons began to broaden when he enrolled at the College of Lewis and Clark. There was no Major League draft and scouts roamed the land looking for talent for their parent clubs. They could wave a contract in front of a young prospect's face and talk him into joining the team, or convince his parents to sign.

"You could really sign with anybody," Ward said. "A Baltimore scout (Don McShane) took an interest in me and just really gave me an opportunity. So I signed with Baltimore."

Ward signed for a $4,000 bonus. The only other team seeking Ward's autograph was Kansas City. To those he attended school with, it must have seemed a bit miraculous that Ward gained any attention at all from professional scouts. When he played second base for the Jefferson High junior varsity, Ward stood 4-foot-9, or 5-2, depending on the source.

"I was a little bitty guy," Ward said. "Entering my senior year I was 5-foot-4. In one year I went from 5-4, 120 pounds to 6 feet, 185. One year. I guess I ate everything. I just had a growth spurt, but it took me so long to get started."

After he grew, Ward found that his swing would knock balls over the fence wherever he went.

"I just never did it when I was little," Ward said. "In the California State League, all of a sudden I was hitting balls over the right-field wall, way over. Then in Appleton, Wisconsin, I played for Earl Weaver and I led the league in hitting. I just didn't think those things were me. I grew into it."

Ward possessed athletic ability, as all professionals do, but neither his style in the field nor on the bases was sandpapered to smoothness. He was no running gazelle, nor was he a vacuum cleaner at third base. Yet he gave his all and when Ward returned to the clubhouse at the end of a game, invariably he wore the dirtiest uniform on the team.

"Pete gets his uniform dirty faster than anybody I've ever seen," long-time White Sox trainer Ed Froelich said of Ward in a 1965 *Sport* magazine article.

Awkwardness defined Ward early in his career. He shifted his batting stance constantly, fidgeting more at the plate than Nomar Garciaparra. Until he corrected his style in the minors, he placed his hands four inches apart on the bat and piled up errors, chiefly on low throws from third base to first. Yet his coaches and managers thought he was going to be an enduring star.

A huge sports fan, Ward not only rooted for the Blackhawks, but worked out with Loyola University's basketball team at a time when the Ramblers were the best college team in the country. And he even spent free time during the baseball season going to other baseball games. After all, the Cubs lived in the same city.

After three years of college ball, where Ward grew in stature and statistics, he still needed a fair amount of seasoning. He spent four years in the Orioles chain and despite future Hall of Famer Brooks Robinson holding down third base for seemingly forever with an anchor heavy enough to hold a battleship still, Ward figured he had a future with Baltimore. At the tail end of the 1962 season, the Orioles brought him up for a look.

"I got called up to Baltimore at the end of the playoffs in AAA and I thought I would be an Oriole," Ward said. "That was my goal in the minors."

Ward appeared in eight games with 21 at-bats. He hit just .143 and before you knew it he was a member of the White Sox.

THE SETTING

On January 14, 1963, the Orioles traded Ward, shortstop Ron Hansen, outfielder Dave Nicholson, and future Hall of Fame pitcher Hoyt Wilhelm to the White Sox for future Hall of Fame shortstop Luis Aparicio and veteran outfielder Al Smith.

There was no third baseman in Ward's way at Comiskey Park and on opening day of the 1963 season Ward was in the White Sox line-up. As careers unfold over the years, with players competing in All-Star games, playoff games, or the World Series, they make memories that last a lifetime. But often players retain vivid memories of their first Major League game or their first game with a new team. There was nothing at stake when Ward suited up for the White Sox. For fans and players alike there was excitement in the air because it was the start of a new season. The winter trade provoked considerable buzz. Aparicio was revered and Smith was appreciated and no one knew what these new guys from Baltimore would bring to the table.

There was considerable pressure on Hansen to perform as the stand-in for Aparicio. Wilhelm was an old pro and a known quantity. In Nicholson, the White Sox were hoping to obtain a useful outfield backup. In Ward the White Sox were buying potential. He was the wild card in the deal. No one, not even Ward, knew how he would perform under the bright lights.

THE GAME OF MY LIFE
BY PETE WARD

CHICAGO WHITE SOX VS. DETROIT TIGERS, APRIL 9, 1963

From a personal standpoint, I'll never forget my first game with the White Sox in 1963 in Detroit. Being on the field when Joel Horlen pitched his no-hitter was a thrill and it came at a real crunch time for us. But from a hitting standpoint, my first game with the White Sox was special. That was opening day in Detroit and I hit a three-run homer in the seventh inning off Jim Bunning to put us ahead. That was a real thrill.

Then, my biggest thrill was that I caught a ball down the line that Al Kaline hit. I made one of the few good plays in my whole career. The ball rolled down the third-base line and I came in and got it. I threw underhand to first base and got him out. That was in the ninth inning. It was a nice way to start out.

So I had a big hit and a big fielding play in my first game for the White Sox. What I tell people is that I started off slowly and tailed off later. But really, you know, it was a good year for all of us involved in the trade. I hit 22 home runs with 84 RBIs and batted .295. Ron Hansen hit pretty well and Dave Nicholson hit 22 home runs, too.

GAME RESULTS

The White Sox defeated the Tigers, 7-5, on the occasion of Ward's debut. Detroit scored four runs in the second inning and led the entire game until Ward smashed his big blast, though the White Sox had scored three runs in the third. The right-handed Bunning, who won more than 100 games in both the American and National Leagues before becoming a U.S. senator from Kentucky, seemed to have the game in control when Ward came up.

Nellie Fox and Floyd Robinson were on base, but the White Sox had two outs and trailed by a run. Ward powdered the ball to give Chicago the lead and the win. Ward had made a strong enough impression on manager Al Lopez to break into the starting lineup, and Lopez gushed about Ward's potential.

"He's good right now," Lopez said a couple of months into Ward's third-base tenure. "But he keeps getting better every day, both at the plate and in the field. The sky seems to be the limit with him. Before he's through, he may become one of the great ones."

Ward reciprocated with his own feelings about Lopez.

"I think I played for two guys that I would say were great managers," Ward recalled later. "One was Al Lopez and the other was Ralph Houk in New York for my last year. I think it's a manager's job to get the most out of their players, and it doesn't really matter how they do it. I think they both had their own ways. Everyone who ever played for Ralph Houk thought they let him down because they all felt they could have done better. Everybody liked playing for Ralph.

"In 1963, in Chicago, we felt like we could win the pennant again. But looking back on it now, I don't think we had the personnel. Including myself. We had good pitching and we were in every game and we had great leadership and I feel we did have a good team. But I don't think we could quite match up with the Yankees."

The White Sox won 94 games, a good measuring stick, but the Yankees were an extraordinary 10½ games better. Ward was a rookie in 1963 and he was surrounded by veteran players, many of whom were key figures from winning the 1959 pennant.

"Nellie was special," Ward said of Fox, the All-Star second baseman. "I knew that before I even thought about going to Chicago. He was a great player and the veterans really welcomed us. Sherm Lollar was a leader on that ballclub. We really did have a good bunch of people."

It was still a bit startling for Ward to realize he was no longer a midget baseball player and more of a stud hitter.

"All of a sudden I'm a 20-home-run man in the majors," he said.

REFLECTIONS ON BASEBALL

Ward's rookie year was his best. He never played as many games or hit as high an average, and he only bettered his home-run total (by one) once. He was a nine-year Major Leaguer, a solid third sacker, but one who never grew into an All-Star—though he became an adept, if reluctant, pinch hitter. Knowledge of the game came through as one of Ward's positive traits, and he was in demand as a minor-league manager for seven years. Among the players he tutored in the minors was future Cy Young-winner LaMarr Hoyt in Des Moines. After that, Ward joined the Atlanta Braves coaching staff for one season in 1978.

"I was the first base coach and the hitting instructor, but I didn't do much hitting instruction," Ward remembered. "I was pretty much just the first base coach. It was great and it was fun to be there and all that, but I didn't mind when I got out of baseball."

Ward entered private business, working for a beer company and starting his own travel agency. He is also a key figure in the annual Hank and Moose golf tournament that was started by ex-players Hank Bauer and Bill Skowron, and has raised about $4 million in Ward's estimation for the local Dornbecker Hospital. The event is one of the highlight reunion dates on the calendar for ex-White Sox, usually attracting Billy Pierce, Gary Peters, and Jim Landis, all flying long distances to be part of it.

Ward offered a "Hell, yes," when asked if he still cheers for the White Sox. He is not one of the ex-players who made it to Chicago to watch the 2005 World Series games, however. He was on a river-boat cruise in Germany at the time.

"Up until I retired, there were two kinds of people I made fun of," he said. "One was golfers and the other was people who went to Starbucks for coffee. And now I do both damned near every day. I figured who would pay $3 for a cup of coffee? I never played golf until I retired. I'm not a good golfer."

A couple of years ago Ward appeared at a sports banquet in New York that serves as a fundraiser for retired players in need when his old teammate Gary Peters needled him.

"He came up to me and said, 'Pete, I understand you're playing a lot of golf.' I said, 'Yeah.' He said, 'Well, you ought to be good. All you have to do is hit it. You don't have to catch it or throw it.'"

The old joke about Ward's fielding persisted, but it was a fair bet that Peters still wouldn't want to pitch to him.

CHAPTER 12

NANCY FAUST

Nancy Faust, a fixture on the organ on the first level at U.S. Cellular Field behind home plate, grew up on the northwest side of Chicago. She attended Roosevelt High School and North Park College. As a youth, Faust was neither a White Sox fan nor a Cubs fan, but she remembers being excited when the White Sox won the pennant in 1959.

"Just because it was Chicago," she remarked. "Other than that, before I got hired to play the organ at games in 1970, I had attended one game."

Faust cannot remember the exact year, but she had a cousin who shared a birthday with Cleveland Indians slugger Rocky Colavito and arranged to have her birthday party at the park when the Indians came to Chicago.

"We just kept yelling, 'Happy birthday, Rocky!' to him," Faust said. "Members of my family were not baseball fans. They were just busy working and not into a lot of recreation."

Faust's mother, Jacqueline, grew up as a talented, all-around musician and became adept at the piano. Faust's mom was the key influence in her taking up the organ.

"She had quite the colorful background in her musical career," Faust said. "Although she never taught me piano, she was always there to help me, and then the organ became such a popular instrument that my mother switched to that, just to get more work, and that's when it captured my fancy. I was about five."

When Faust was in college, majoring in psychology, many of her friends were sports fans, but it still did not take with her. They were, however, aware that she could play songs upon request and if an instrument was around it was request time for Nancy.

"They would say, 'Play this song,' and I could play it because I have a good ear," Faust said. "I wasn't, I still am not, like my mother, a good sight reader, so I couldn't be a music major. I played by ear, but my friends who were avid sports fans encouraged me and helped me write letters to some of the teams. They thought it was a good avenue for me to get a job—and a good avenue for them to see a complimentary game. And it worked."

One day Nancy filled in for her mother at a luncheon attended by White Sox team management, including general manager Stu Holcomb. Her repertoire featured such songs as "Moon River" and "Alley Cat."

"Andy Williams was very popular and when I was in college I'd fill in for my mother on jobs playing for dinners," Faust said. "I would play a lot of Andy Williams and a lot of songs from *The Sound of Music*. I did a lot of those kind of songs. *My Fair Lady*. And *Oklahoma*, *West Side Story*. I knew all the songs from Broadway musicals in those days. *My Fair Lady* was probably the first show I ever knew. I did a lot of music where you played dinner music while people were eating."

Holcomb heard Faust play and called her. Playing essentially background music for people who were at a dinner served Faust well. The organist at the ballpark performs basically the same function. The crowd is present for baseball, but clues into the short periods of music before games, between innings, the seventh-inning stretch, or when a player comes to bat.

THE SETTING

Despite the longevity of Nancy Faust's baseball career playing the organ at White Sox games, she had never played at the World Series.

She was hired in 1970, and the last time the White Sox had been in a Series was 1959. It was a long dry spell between that year and 2005 for White Sox fans, but Faust was still working for the team, had been playing her tunes for 35 years when the White Sox had their breakthrough in 2005, winning the American League pennant and the world championship.

Because Faust was a musician first and a sports fan second, it was easy for her to focus on her job without being distracted by events on the field. She had to be aware of things in order to make sure she played the organ at appropriate times, but she never became a human box score able to recite game details.

"I have to follow it closely because I can't interrupt or interfere with the action," she said. "Everything I play, when I do play, reflects something that's happened in the game. But I don't have the kind of brain that a lot of baseball fans have."

Initially, too timid to do anything but follow very explicit playing instructions, Faust's maturation on the job and acquired wisdom about the sport led her to branch out in her play list. She asked for permission to shape her own version of the "Charge!" cheer, and Faust, who played while encased in a glass cage of sorts where she could only wave to fans, requested that the door to her booth be left open. She encouraged fans to stick their heads in and say hello.

"I kind of got more bold as time went on and more confident and got greater suggestions from the fans," Faust said. "They enlighten me still. There was a character in *The Andy Griffith Show,* and it was the same name as a player who was coming up to bat. I wouldn't have known this, but a fan told me. That's the kind of thing that makes me look good."

Of course, Faust played "Take Me Out to the Ballgame" regularly. It was legendary broadcaster Harry Caray, during his stint with the Sox before joining the Cubs, who gave Faust a public identity. When the seventh inning rolled around Caray yelled into his microphone, "Come on, Nancy!" She also hit a stretch where she played "Forever in Blue Jeans" frequently. Years later, fans still come up to her and say, "I remember the old days. You would play 'Forever in Blue Jeans.'"

"And that reminded them of baseball," Faust said. "You kind of set your own standard, I guess. I had the good fortune of being located where I interacted so much with the fans."

When Faust got the job playing the organ for the White Sox, she was pleased. She was 23 and employed coming out of college. Her measurement of success in an unfamiliar venue was simple.

"I just thought if I could be hired back for a second year I could prove that I wasn't a total flop," she said.

The perky, friendly, attractive blonde woman who works for a baseball team never became a baseball fan in the sense of recounting play-by-play in casual conversation, though she certainly knows a lot more about the game than she did in college.

"I became a White Sox fan," Faust said. "Sure you want to see them do well. You don't bite the hand that feeds you and you share the excitement of the fans. My job was always more fun when the team was doing well."

THE GAME OF MY LIFE
BY NANCY FAUST

CHICAGO WHITE SOX VS. HOUSTON ASTROS, OCTOBER 22, 2005, WORLD SERIES GAME 1

There was a sense of pride going to the park. I got there really early. The time before a game is great for me because I'm actually able to finish or complete a song as the fans enter the park. A whole song. Whenever a game is scheduled to start, I start playing an hour earlier—until the annoucements are made. Really only steadily for a half-hour and then here and there.

To get ready for the game I worked up really good renditons of the *Star Wars* theme and "All-Star." I was just excited to be part of it. There were definitely a few years of waiting for that moment. It could well have been a once-in-a-lifetime shot. It was very exciting, but the other emotion I felt was extreme sadness for those who weren't around anymore who were such great fans for a long time. It's hard to talk about it without choking up. Gosh, those people who just missed out on what would have been the thrill of a lifetime.

Every year, ticket holders stopped by. I have so many regulars. And every year there are people who pass away and I know about it. I just hear a lot of stories in my booth from the people themselves, or people's friends. There's always somebody. During last season somebody came by and said their relative's name was Sven, I think, and they described him and I think I knew who he was. They said, "He always came to your booth." He died of diabetes. I went to the *Chicago Tribune* obituaries and I found him. Sure enough, in the obit it said, "Big White Sox fan."

I think my purpose being there now goes beyond playing. Having the organ there is a kind of constant. I don't know how else to describe it, but it's been through a lot of sadness, a lot of good times, through generations. And the best time of all was the World Series in Chicago.

GAME RESULTS

The White Sox won the first World Series game played in Chicago in 46 years by a score of 5-3, the first victory in a four-game sweep of the Astros. In spite of such a long wait, when the Series ended in four straight games, Chicago lost out on hosting additional contests. Not that the fans seemed to mind. The parade the city threw to honor the team might have attracted up to two million supporters. Faust was invited to play her organ at the celebration, and she said that might have been even more fun than being at the World Series opener.

"I think I was the most emotional when I was attending the rally," Faust said. "When we were setting up the organ the streets were just lined with happy fans. It was just so heartwarming that something great had happened and so many people turned out and they were all so orderly. I was so proud."

As part of the big downtown party, Faust played "Na Na Hey Hey Kiss Him Goodbye" (she takes the credit for provoking Sox fans into chanting the song when opposing pitchers are knocked out of the box), "Don't Stop Believing" (the Journey song that became emblematic of the White Sox's pennant run), and "Go-Go White Sox."

Faust was one of the longtime employees honored to receive a World Series ring from owner Jerry Reinsdorf—in Faust's opinion, the best commemorative souvenir possible.

"The current management has been wonderful to me," Faust said. "Jerry has just been wonderful to his employees."

One day during the lead-up to the Series, when Chicago was going ga-ga, Faust picked up her telephone and was invited to perform with the Chicago Symphony. She said she thought it was a prank call, but it was a genuine invitation.

REFLECTING ON BASEBALL

Faust said she looks at her organ-playing song choices as being family oriented. What makes fans in the know chuckle is how she might nail a player's demeanor or name in a single bar of music. Sammy Sosa, who briefly played with the Sox before attaining stardom with the Cubs, was a player she felt was a hot dog. So Faust played the "Oscar Meyer Wiener" song. Former player Pete Incaviglia often heard the strains of "In-A-Gadda-Da-Vida." And Faust was always inspired by Tim Salmon, sometimes teasing him with the theme from *Jaws* or the song from the Charlie the Tuna commercial. Trot Nixon, once an outfielder with the Red Sox, now with Cleveland, has been greeted with "Hail to the Chief." It helps to be a quick thinker if you're a fan, because Faust sure is. She says most of what she does is spur of the moment.

Faust, who is married with a son and is the owner of five acres of land populated by chickens and other animals, made a spur-of-the-moment decision years ago that still affects her life. Bill Veeck, the creative marketing genius who twice owned the White Sox, had a giveaway of oddball prizes one day. Adventure Land, an amusement park, had donated an elderly donkey to a fundraising cause, but the fan who won never claimed it. Faust had a barn and space so she asked Veeck if she could take the animal home.

"He let me have the donkey," Faust said. "I had the donkey another 10 years until it died. I look back at it (Veeck's tenure) as a wacky time."

Like the timely Chicago Symphony gig, Faust's name-recognition from the ballpark has attracted further notice. A Chicago advertising agency handling the McDonald's account signed Faust during a promotion. Among their four selections was Faust's version of "Take Me Out to the Ballgame."

After a nearly quarter-century-long playing streak, Faust's role for the White Sox has been reduced. She plays just afternoon games these days, less than 30 a season. There are more promotions than ever—advertising gimmicks and video scoreboard games that fill time between innings—so Faust is used less.

"I'm 60 now, so I think my time is winding down," Faust said. "I hope to always attend games, but I don't know how much."

As a young psychology major and musician, Faust never expected to work out of a ballpark. People plan lives, but life takes them in other directions. Faust's oldest friends and relatives can't believe her life turned out this way.

"It's been such an evolution," Faust said of her non-baseball years. "There are people that knew me then and probably think the whole thing is crazy. But there are fans who will come by and say, 'What do you have to pay to get a job like this? Do you pay the park?' They just can't believe somebody is getting paid to do something this glamorous. I guess I didn't think it would become a lifetime career. I had no such aspirations. If you told me when I was 23 that I would be there when I was 40, let alone 60, I'd say, 'Forget it.' It just evolved."

Donkeys, chickens, and family aside, the Chicago White Sox and baseball became much more important to her than Nancy Faust ever could have imagined.

"It's just been an integral part of my life and defined my life," Faust said. "It defined my relationships with friends. It seems like all my best friends have been made through the ballpark, as well as so many acquaintances."

If you give her a moment to consider, Faust will probably come up with an appropriate song to describe those thoughts. Perhaps Frank Sinatra singing, "My Kind of Town."

CHAPTER 13

BILL MELTON

Bill Melton's dad, Ed, was a chief petty officer in the Navy during World War II and when the war ended he was stationed at a naval base in Gulfport, Mississippi, teaching an engineering course. This would be where Melton was born in 1945. As a navy man, Ed Melton was transferred often. After Mississippi, the family lived in New England and then moved to California—first to San Diego, and then on to other communities. Except for his time on the Gulf Coast as an infant, Melton spent no time in Mississippi beyond a trip nearly 30 years ago. Ironically (and he gets a kick out of his inclusion), when *Sports Illustrated* chose a state-by-state all-athletic team a few years ago, Melton was selected.

"I'm on the All-Mississippi team," Melton laughed.

The criteria involved choosing athletes based on where they were born. Melton's first athletic love was not baseball. He played Little League in California, but he was as involved in basketball and football. Melton's first professional baseball game was as a fan with his father in 1959—none other than one of the World Series encounters at the Los Angeles Coliseum between the Dodgers and White Sox. The Meltons sat so far away from the field that they could have used a telescope to watch the batters. Melton was 14 and far from filled out. Perhaps that's why he identified with the littlest White Sox infielders.

"I liked Luis Aparicio and Nellie Fox because they looked only about an inch tall from where I was sitting in front of the clock out there," Melton said.

A few years later, Melton was attending Citrus Junior College, working to get his grades up for a transfer to a larger school like San Diego State to study engineering when Hollis "Sloppy" Thurston, a long-time White Sox scout, saw him play ball. The World Series observation had converted Melton into a White Sox fan—life's foreshadowing since he actually got to play alongside Aparicio in the Sox infield.

As he considered his future in engineering, Melton signed up to play weekend ball on a friend's team that gathered in Pasadena in a high-caliber league that featured many minor-league players. On one of his finest hitting days, Melton slugged three home runs. Thurston happened to be in attendance.

"Basically, he called me over from the dugout and asked me if I wanted to sign with the White Sox," Melton said. "I said, 'Well, I need a summer job.' That's how I thought of it, as a summer job. I was 17 and I wanted to become a mechanical engineer. He said, 'We can only pay you $6,000.' I just hemmed and hawed. I didn't know what I wanted to do."

Melton's was not the typical reason baseball-loving teens sign.

"The long and the short of it is that I needed money for books," Melton said. "I went into baseball for school. I never had any intention of making the big leagues—no desire, no nothing."

Melton was assigned to the White Sox farm club.

"I was making like $450 a month," he said. "That was a lot of money. It was a great summer job. There were 63 players and 58 of them were released after two months there. The next year I came back and played Class A ball in the Florida State League."

Melton kept making the cut and kept Sox management's eye on him as he moved to Appleton, Wisconsin, and Knoxville, Tennessee. In 1968, the White Sox kept him around Chicago for 34 games and in 1969 he stuck for good.

"The reason I probably made it, I tell everybody when I do my speeches and stuff around the city, is that there was no pressure on me," Melton said. "There were All-Americans from Michigan and all of these big schools. I was from a little school. I never was an All-American. I was a little intimidated, but once I figured out I was as good as them, the confidence started coming. I never even went to big-league training camp all of those years. The only year I got invited was the last year and the next year I was in the big leagues."

Melton fell into baseball. He hadn't dreamed about becoming a Major Leaguer and he was loose, knowing if he didn't make it he could go back to school and train in engineering.

"It was all about no pressure," he said. "The pressure started when I got to that big-league camp when I was 21 and every one of those guys was a veteran. Again, you know what? I started thinking, 'I'm as good as these guys.' I really started believing that if I practiced hard I would be as good as those guys."

Of course, Melton had been an outfielder and he was being converted to third base, so the learning curve was tougher than it had been at Citrus Junior College.

"You know, you take a lot of beatings, but by the time you come out of it, you hope to get recognition because it's very frustrating," Melton said.

THE SETTING

The Chicago White Sox had never been a power-hitting team. They had been "The Hitless Wonders" and the "Go-Go White Sox" in different decades, but home run hitters were a rare species on the South side of Chicago. The Yankees had gone from Babe Ruth and Lou Gehrig to Joe DiMaggio and Mickey Mantle and Roger Maris. The Red Sox had Ted Williams for more than two decades. Every team had somebody who could pulverize the ball. The White Sox used to excel on the base paths, stealing their runs one at a time. The club had never had a player lead the league in homers, dating back 70 years.

From a remarkable, fan-pleasing season of 1961, when Maris stroked 61 homers to break Babe Ruth's single-season mark and Mantle was on his shoulder with 54 blasts, home-run hitting suffered a decline. It was apparent as the 1971 season approached its conclusion that someone was going to lead the American League in homers with 30-something. A low 30-something. Bill Melton was in the mix. So was Reggie Jackson, who was still with the Oakland A's. And so was Norm Cash, the first baseman traded away from the White Sox a decade earlier who created such a fine career with the Detroit Tigers. Also, Reggie Smith of the Red Sox was lurking in the shadows.

Coming into the final two games of the regular season, Melton had 30 home runs. With everybody still playing, someone was bound to get hot and become the king of swat. The standings were settled, so last-minute slugging was not going to affect the teams. Whoever won the home run crown was doing it for pride.

"There was no free agency, no nothing, it was just something I needed to do," Melton said. "But at the same time I wasn't trying to hit home runs, making it probably an easier approach."

THE GAMES OF MY LIFE
BY BILL MELTON

CHICAGO WHITE SOX VS. MILWAUKEE BREWERS, SEPTEMBER 29 AND SEPTEMBER 30, 1971

I've been asked about a thousand times about leading the league in home runs. "How did you do it?" That's the question fans always ask. There was just a 24-hour period in there at the end of the season covering the last two games that stands out.

We were playing the Milwaukee Brewers—that was before they moved to the National League. On the next-to-last night of the season, I hit two home runs off pitcher Jim Slaton. Slaton pitched a good game, but we were ahead by two runs early. Both runs scored on solo home runs by me. I hit a home run in the first inning with nobody out. Then I hit a home run in the third inning with two outs. At the end of the game I had 32 home runs and I was tied for the American

League lead. Jackson, whose season ended that day with him going 0-for-5, and Cash, whose season also ended that day, each had 32 as well.

When I had been out in Oakland, some members of the A's said Jackson was breaking out in hives, and I was asking what for. He was nervous about leading the league. For a guy like that, who lives by marketing and did very well for himself in it, that was very important. Apparently he went to the hospital for four or five days for hives. I don't know, maybe if I'd thought about baseball the way he did I probably would have lasted longer. To him it was more important. The only big promoter in baseball in the 1970s was Reggie Jackson. That was the funniest thing about the whole thing. He was the only guy that deep into the marketing. Now it's everybody. I didn't ever have any endorsements. Reggie was way, way ahead of the game and he was doing national stuff. I don't have a problem with that. To me it was another day when I played. Jackson said something in a newspaper as the season was ending about the home run race—"Now we'll separate the men from the boys."

I celebrated with the guys that night and we might not have got in till four or five in the morning. And we had a day game the next day—I think we started at 11 a.m. or noon. Boy, it was hot. But I got up there in the third inning and I hit my 33rd homer off Bill Parsons and that gave me the home run championship. That 24 hours is the thing I hear about the most.

GAME RESULTS

Chicago won both games by the same 2-1 score and the fans of the White Sox did not exactly pack the place. Paid attendance for the next-to-last game of the season at Comiskey Park was 5,106. Paid attendance on the last day was 2,814—good seats still available.

Manager Chuck Tanner batted Melton leadoff to give him more of a chance at an extra at-bat and hence a possible bonus chance to hit a homer. His first time up against Parsons, a 90-mph fastball broke Melton's bat. He looked into the dugout to see his joke-playing teammates placing a towel over the cracked bat and giving it last rites.

Melton said he was on a plane to California by late afternoon of the final game, but he believes there would have been much of a hullabaloo if he led the American League in homers today.

"If I was to be playing today I'd probably have milked it for all I could," Melton said. "But it was really just a function of being part of a team that was really bad and was starting to come back and play better baseball. We were a young team in 1971. It was an accomplishment that the team was better than it was the year before.

"It is not hard to picture using the home run title to say to general manager Roland Hemond, 'You've got to pay me a lot of money.' But I don't think that was the mind-set in those days. The more I sat at home over the winter, though, I understood the accomplishment because it was the first time a White Sox player had ever led the league."

It was surprising that the Sox had never had such a player.

"It was an amazing thing," Melton said. "When I sat back and thought about it, I went, 'Wow.' As time goes on, the park's changed and everything's different. I was the White Sox home run leader for their first 80 years or so. Harold Baines passed me in the mid-1980s and I've fallen further than that now. But at least I led it."

That season was the best all-around campaign of Melton's career, with 86 RBIs and his most games played. Melon cut down on strikeouts (he once struck out 11 times in a row in the majors) and errors in the field. Only a year before, he was becoming a national source of interest for sloppy fielding—he committed 10 errors in the White Sox' first 24 games. On one play, Melton had to be carried off the field on a stretcher spurting blood from his nose because a ball hit him in the face. Melton had great difficulty adjusting to artificial turf and the way balls seemed to pick up speed when they skidded off it.

"That rug has got me psyched," he said when things were at their worst. "I just can't handle it. Those balls just whiz by."

But Melton worked to correct his shortcomings and got better. The year of his top-flight slugging, Melton's fielding percentage was

.0001 better than the legendary Brooks Robinson's at third. After his 33-homer season, Melton joked that it "was the best-kept secret in baseball." Given that *New York Times* sports columnist Arthur Daley wrote, "Who the hell is Bill Melton?" he may have had a point. But in Chicago he had earned the nickname "Beltin' Melton." He hit three home runs in a game against the Seattle Pilots in 1969 and also doubled that day. That was belting 'em.

Unfortunately, he could not follow up his 1971 season with one to match in 1972. A back injury put Melton on the shelf for all but 57 games. When he returned the next year and played well, he won the American League Comeback Player of the Year award with 20 homers and 87 RBIs. Melton improved his back with experimental treatments rather than surgery and got a lot of attention for that until he stepped back into the box and began slamming homers again.

REFLECTIONS ON BASEBALL

Melton retired from baseball in 1977 after his 10th season, but has had a long and satisfying career in broadcasting. He may be white-haired, but Melton is still around the White Sox almost as much as he was when he played. Between radio pregame and postgame shows, and analysis for Comcast in Chicago, Melton has been on the air for 17 years. Melton never did become a mechanical engineer. Broadcasting is fun, but playing baseball for a living can't be topped.

"Never," Melton said. "It's never as much fun doing broadcasting as it was playing. But I'm very fortunate to be able to sit up in a booth and watch the team I've been a fan of for 50 years, to watch them play, to watch players develop, to watch the season."

The Sox were going through a dismal 2007 when Melton spoke, but he said the failure of that club couldn't outweigh the pleasures others provided.

"I've really had too many good years to worry about one year," he said. "This is something that's almost surreal. I've never seen a collapse like this. I've been with these guys for a long time. Such a good team should have won 95 games and the same team couldn't break .500. It's very disappointing. I've never got to the studio when I had to be on the set in the eighth inning and put the microphone and earpiece on to get ready for the cameras after the last three outs and got punched in the gut watching that bullpen so often."

Melton still bleeds after defeats like a White Sox regular and it makes sense. When he's not watching the Sox play he's on the job for the team roaming around the community. He joins Minnie Minoso, Bill Skowron, and Ron Kittle doing everything from visiting season ticket-holders in the U.S. Cellular suites to speaking at luncheons and banquets and visiting team-sponsored baseball camps.

"My summer is booked," Melton said. "I do as much off the air as on the air."

The main difference between Melton in the 2000s and Melton in the 1970s with the White Sox is he used to wear No. 14 on his jersey. Now he wears a suit.

CHAPTER 14

GREG WALKER

Where Greg Walker grew up in the Deep South in the 1960s, football was king. College football ruled the landscape and high school football rated right behind it. That pecking order was true in the Georgia town where Walker was raised, which was fine with him since football was also first in Walker's heart. Douglas is a medium-sized town in southern Georgia where, before the Atlanta Falcons and later the Jacksonville Jaguars came along, there was no pro team to swear allegiance to. Walker was a quarterback in football.

"A slow quarterback," he added.

And he was a catcher for the baseball team. However, playing football ended up dramatically affecting his baseball career. During a game, a defensive player smashed into Walker helmet-first and bashed his throwing shoulder. After that he never had the same velocity.

"I turned into a very poor thrower the rest of my career," Walker said.

Walker never thought he had a big future in football because of his lack of foot speed, but he had to adjust to the injury in order to advance his baseball career.

"I grew up a catcher," the 6-foot-3, 210-pound Walker said. "After I tore up my arm I ended up moving to first base. I had never really played first. For a long time after that I never really had a lot of confidence in my fielding."

Even in the minors, Walker felt if he was going to advance it was going to be because of his hitting.

"I was a guy who was hurt my whole career," he said. "I had not been a top prospect. I kind of made myself a prospect. I was a poor defensive player."

Walker said nobody pushed him to become a professional athlete, no one demanded he practice or produce. But the worthy advice his father passed on, he said, was general advice that could apply to any boy looking ahead to a career in any field—"Go about my business the right way. Come to work every day and earn your money."

Living a couple of hundred miles from Atlanta, Walker said he never took road trips to watch the Major League Braves when he was young.

"I saw one big-league game before I played in one," he said.

THE SETTING

There was a grand feeling of optimism in the White Sox spring training camp of 1983. The team was coming off a respectable 87-75 season, only six games out of first place in the American League Western Division. In a refreshing outlook for a team that had experienced mostly suffer-along seasons for decades, one thing was apparent—the team was going to try out a new first baseman.

Walker had been called up at the end of the 1982 season for his Major-League debut. He played in 11 games and though he came to bat only 17 times, he stroked seven hits. That meant he could spend the winter in the reflected glow of a .412 batting average. It was enough of a showing to make the organization think about him, too, and he won the starting job in spring training. No one—least of all Walker—expected him to bat .412 over the course of a season. But management liked the looks of Walker at the plate and plugged him in at first, even as he worried about the quality of his fielding. He had never quite regained the sureness with the glove that he had felt with a catcher's mitt on his paw.

Yet when the 1983 season opened, Walker was in the starting lineup to play against the Rangers at Arlington Stadium. As it turned out, Walker was glad that the ballgame was played just about as far from Chicago as possible. Walker was fifth in the batting order, an indication that manager Tony La Russa had confidence in him. What Walker did not anticipate was his first game of the new season (his first as a full-time starter) turning into a nightmare—though a life-changing one.

THE GAME OF MY LIFE
(AS A PLAYER)

BY GREG WALKER

CHICAGO WHITE SOX VS. TEXAS RANGERS, APRIL 4, 1983

One of my most special moments playing that year was a bad memory. I didn't think I was going to make the team in 1983 and there I was starting on opening day. It's pretty well known that White Sox fans can be hard on you if you make mistakes, so it was a good thing the game was in Texas. I made two errors in the first inning of my first big-league game as a regular. Defense. You can't imagine how it feels. I thought my career was over right then. We lost the game, too. I swung the bat pretty good, but I learned a lot from my mistakes. We had a little team get-together that night. Some veterans really spent a lot of quality time with me and told me exactly what I needed to be told.

Jerry Koosman (a 222-game winner) and Greg Luzinski (a 307 home-run man), guys who had been around, both of them grabbed me and basically said, "Don't feel sorry for yourself. Go out there and show them that you can play."

Right then I could have shriveled up and been sent back to AAA, but instead of that happening, they helped me up my game and turn that year around, taking a negative and turning it into a positive. The easy thing would have been to feel sorry for myself and end up getting shipped back to the minors.

Koosman and Luzinski were telling me that it's a long season and you have to believe in yourself. The easiest thing would have been for me to say, "It's not my time." They grabbed me by the throat and said, "Toughen up. Let's go. Go play the game. We believe in you."

Jerry Koosman and (future Hall of Fame catcher) Carlton Fisk, they were some of the greatest competitors of all time and they were saying they believed in me and were pulling for me. That's one of the reasons I do what I do now (coaching) because I know that these guys taught me some things and it's a pleasure to pass along some of those things from time to time.

GAME RESULTS

Texas won 5-3, and two unearned runs in that first inning contributed. However, before he made the miscues with the glove, Walker had been to bat, and as part of a White Sox three-run rally in the top of the first, he smashed a triple that drove in a run.

The contrasting situations summed up the state of Walker's career at the time. The White Sox knew he could hit, but they wondered if his glove would be too much of a liability. And if fielding was such a problem, should he stay with the big club, or be farmed out to concentrate on improving glove work?

"It was really being talked about a lot," Walker said. "If I wasn't going to play a lot, they felt they should send me to AAA. This was going on during the first month of the season."

About two weeks after Walker booted the two balls, the White Sox were playing the Detroit Tigers. Dan Petry was on the mound for Detroit in a close game when Walker was inserted as a pinch hitter. Walker smashed a home run in the eighth inning, the White Sox won 3-1, and it may have been a career-saving hit.

"After that," Walker said, "Tony (La Russa) told me, 'You know what? We're a better team with you on this team. I'm keeping you. I'm not going by the tradition of "he's young, he needs to play." We have a good team. We want to win and we're better with you here.' So I got to stay there."

The White Sox won 99 games and played the Baltimore Orioles for the American League title.

"I started the fourth game of the championship series, and even though we ended up losing, it was a real exciting thing to be in the playoffs," Walker said.

THE GAME OF MY LIFE
(AS A COACH)

BY GREG WALKER

CHICAGO WHITE SOX VS. HOUSTON ASTROS, OCTOBER 26, 2005

The game that sticks out, without a doubt, is the last game of the World Series. I guess that's no surprise. When it came down to that last play and our shortstop Juan Uribe made a great play, I was actually looking down at the scorecard to see who was coming up for Houston because I thought they'd tied the game.

And then I'm looking out of the corner of my eye and I see him field the ball and I say, "It's over." Really, up until that second it was so intense and there was so much involved and so much on the line that we felt if we lost the game we might lose the momentum. Every game, every out, was so important during the World Series that when it was over, it was stunning. It was over, but it didn't sink in right away. I had tried to win a World Series as a player and never came really close.

GAME RESULTS

The White Sox swept Houston in the 2005 World Series, but though the overall result was a blowout, all of the games were close and Walker had every reason to worry in the fourth game. The Sox won the games—5-3, 7-6, 7-5 in 14 innings, and 1-0. In the final game, Uribe dove into the stands along the left-field line for the second out and then scooped up a grounder and threw to first for the last out.

Walker is very proud of the World Series ring he earned and rather than keep it in a glass case or tuck it away out of sight, he wears it often. During the 2007 season, when the White Sox were struggling, even with many of the same players who had brought the city the championship, Walker said he kept wearing the bauble that was emblematic of success.

"I wear it right now to remind myself that we're still pretty good," he said.

REFLECTIONS ON BASEBALL

There were many reasons why Walker appreciated winning a World Series crown. He strove for one as a player. He shared the coaching duties on a staff where most of the guys knew each other for years. And also because he felt glad to be alive.

In late July during the 1988 season, Walker was on the field at Comiskey Park for White Sox warmups a couple of hours before a game with the California Angels. All of a sudden, Walker keeled over, collapsing on the field and stunning his teammates. Trainer Herm Schneider was urgently summoned. After a quick examination of Walker, who was experiencing convulsions and shifting in and out of consciousness, Schneider had to reach surgical scissors down the player's throat to prevent him from swallowing his own tongue. At the time, Schneider thought Walker might be choking on chewing gum or tobacco.

Walker was rushed to the hospital. He thought he'd had a heart attack at age 29. The diagnosis was a seizure of undetermined origin. While in the hospital, Walker suffered a second seizure. The doctors didn't know why, but concluded that the seizures were caused by a virus in the brain. The seizures were also symptomatic of epilepsy.

However, after some rest, treatment, and medication, Walker rebounded and resumed his baseball career, playing parts of two more seasons, though not as productively because of a serious shoulder injury. Walker credits Schneider with saving his life.

"I was purple. I was blue. I was this far from death," Walker said while describing the situation for a newspaper years ago, holding his hands only six inches apart. "I don't think it's stretching it to say Herm saved my life."

Hampered by the shoulder problem, Walker was disappointed that he could not leave baseball on his own terms. He returned to Georgia and went into private business, doing well in the fields of home medical equipment and food brokerage. But when he got the chance to return to baseball in 2002 with AAA Charlotte, Walker found the idea appealing. He joined the coaching staff put together by his old teammate Ozzie Guillen when he became White Sox manager and in 2007 completed his fourth season as a Sox coach.

"I've had a lot of fun being a coach," Walker reflected. "To be my age and still be in uniform and in competition with a sport I love—with a team I love—it's a dream job."

CHAPTER 15

ERIC SODERHOLM

The Minnesota Twins discovered Eric Soderholm while he was playing baseball for South Georgia Junior College in Douglas, Georgia. After being born in upstate New York, Soderholm played high school ball in the weather-friendly confines of Miami. Competing for Miami Coral Park High School under the tutelage of respected coach Red Berry, Soderholm blossomed as a player. Berry, who operates baseball camps, had a good eye for talent and wrote letters to colleges on Soderholm's behalf.

Scouts glancing at Soderholm on the field were just as likely to look away because the player's build did not inspire confidence. He had a big-leaguer's heart and improving skills, but looked more like a kid starting high school than finishing it. Four-year baseball powers in the South were not going to spend scholarship money on Soderholm at that stage of his development.

"I was 145, 150 pounds soaking wet and had not come into my own yet," Soderholm said. "So there was not going to be a four-year scholarship to a University of Florida or some other big school. It was just out of the question. Coach Berry said, 'It would be better for you to go to junior college and start building up a little bit.'"

Coach knew best: as soon as he entered junior college, Soderholm began putting more muscle on his bones and adding power.

"I don't know if it was the Georgia grits or what, but I started filling out," Soderholm said. "I went from 145, 150 to 165, 170 and I promise you it wasn't steroids or drug-induced. I just matured. I just started filling out my body and those little line drives I was hitting over the shortstop's head were now going to the warning track and I was starting to hit the ball out of the park."

It was the Twins who recognized the new and improved Soderholm model and made him their No. 1 draft pick in the 1968 supplemental draft.

"Then, boom, I was a pro baseball player," Soderholm said. "Quite honestly, as a kid growing up I loved playing, but I never really had dreams of becoming a Major League player."

Soderholm was a baseball fan like other kids, absorbing much of what he knew about the sport from broadcast games. He remembers the home run battle of 1961 between Roger Maris and Mickey Mantle, and he knew he was a good player for the neighborhood, but never thought of himself becoming a player on par with the guys on TV.

"I was always the first kid picked for the Little League teams," Soderholm said, "but I was playing because I loved it. In junior high, my coach started talking to me about people coming around to watch me play. I think there were some scouts coming around in high school, but that was kept hush hush."

Soderholm suspects that Berry wanted to him to remain grounded, but that wasn't a problem.

"I truly didn't think I was that good," Soderholm said. "I was a decent player. Then the next thing, all of a sudden, bing, I'm popping the ball out of the park and I'm drafted by the Twins. I go, 'Whoa, shoot, I'm being offered a contract to sign pro!' I was shocked. I just never thought of myself as being that good and, boom, I worked my way through the minor leagues."

When fans think of Minnesota Twins history they often recall greats like Rod Carew, Harmon Killebrew, and Tony Oliva. Soderholm thought those were the truly talented guys and yet he was a fellow traveler.

"I always had a good work ethic, though," Soderholm said. "I was one of those players that wasn't blessed with the same skills as those guys. I had some talent, but the only way I belonged there was to put in the extra work. I was always working harder than the next guy to be the best I could be. I tried different things throughout my career to help. I tried hypnosis. That's well documented. I was one of the first people to introduce hypnosis to baseball."

Hypnosis was not going to make Soderholm bat 1.000, but he could use it for other purposes. "Focus, concentration, confidence," he said. "You know it can get a little bit intimidating up there. You walk into the clubhouse and there's Killebrew, Carew, and Oliva, and you have to think, 'I put my pants on the same way these guys do.' I learned about positive thinking, took a course on motivation, and I saw a dietician-nutritionist."

Soderholm made the Twins roster in 1971, but was a part-time player for three seasons. He became a regular in 1974 and gave Minnesota two solid seasons of infield play with a reliable bat, hitting in the .270s and .280s. Unfortunately, he missed the 1976 season with a devastating knee injury and it was believed his career might be over. Even worse, he was no longer under contract, so it was not clear if any team would even take a chance on him when he was healthy again.

THE SETTING

Soderholm wrecked his left knee. It was more the type of injury that a football player would suffer when a whole team fell on him. There was ligament damage, cartilage damage, and damage to the kneecap.

"It was just a bunch of things all together," Soderholm said. "I needed total reconstruction."

Two surgeries followed. Soderholm then worked like a demon to fix his knee and return to baseball. At a time when weightlifting for baseball players was still frowned on, he turned to Nautilus. He became so devoted to the program and the effect he felt it had in aid-ing his recovery that Soderholm even filmed a promotion for the equipment and displayed it prominently in a movie about his return to baseball. When he wrote a book called *Conditioning for Baseball,* Nautilus was an essential ingredient.

After his struggles, Soderholm was ready to get back into baseball for the 1977 season. It was the fledgling days of free agency and he hoped for an offer from someone. The White Sox, in the form of owner Bill Veeck and general manager Roland Hemond, came calling.

"Bill offered me double the salary I was making with Calvin Griffith and the Twins, so it was a no-brainer to pick Chicago," Soderholm said of the $55,000 deal. "I'll never forget, just before I signed, meeting Roland in his office. I said, 'I just want to go out on the field. I want to stand on third base.' A two-foot snowstorm had hit Chicago that day. I trudged through the snow and stood at third base and looked around. I just wanted to see and feel if it was all right. It felt right. I signed the contract and went over to the hospital to meet Bill Veeck, who was in there for emphysema. And there he is with his wooden leg with the ashtray in it propped up on a pillow."

The men had a pleasant chat and hit it off. Veeck told Soderholm that the club needed a solid infielder and that the White Sox were glad to have him on the team. Soderholm said, "Mr. Veeck, I've worked so hard I'm not going to be a goof. I'm going to be your third baseman and have a big year for you." And Veeck replied, "Son, if you do that, then you come see me at the end of the year and I'll take good care of you."

What neither knew was that the White Sox had put together a special team for the 1977 season, with a mixture of hungry ballplayers like Soderholm and rent-a-player sluggers like Richie Zisk and Oscar Gamble in the final year of their contracts trying to attract long-term deals in free agency. The chemistry was superb, the talent was there, and the atmosphere was just right for a joy ride of a season and the christening of these one-year wonders as "The South Side Hit Men." It was a team White Sox fans would always recall with smiles on their faces.

THE GAME OF MY LIFE
BY ERIC SODERHOLM

CHICAGO WHITE SOX VS. KANSAS CITY ROYALS, JULY 30, 1977

There was a series in July playing the Kansas City Royals that I always remember. We were playing good baseball and people were starting to look at us differently. Nobody had expected the White Sox to do anything that season, but we were winning and I was hitting. Comiskey Park was sold out. It was a big series. The fans had come to realize there was something about this team and they just had a great time cheering for us and singing and chanting.

In this game I went three-for-four with two runs scored and three runs batted in. I hit a huge home run in the seventh inning off Doug Bird, who was pitching for the Royals, that helped us win the game. I remember hitting it and when I ran around the bases it felt like I was just floating because the energy in the stadium was so huge. Everybody was going crazy. We were in a pennant race and the fans were clued into what we could be. They were singing that song, "Na Na Hey Hey Kiss Him Goodbye." The fans cheered so long for hits that you did the old thing where you came out of the dugout and tipped your hat. It was unheard of at the time.

Other teams had been calling us "bush," especially Kansas City, and the fans didn't like that. With all the showmanship and the fans at Comiskey, the other teams thought we were showing them up. So for me to hit a big home run and to beat them was quite memorable.

The South Side Hit Men. People still talk about that team around here.

GAME RESULTS

The White Sox beat the Royals 6-4 that day. The White Sox won 90 games that season a year after finishing last in the Western Division with 54 wins, but that was good enough only for third place when Kansas City won 102 games and Texas 94. Both recorded big late-season winning streaks as the White Sox ran out of gas.

Soderholm, healthy again, fulfilled his promise to Veeck, playing in 130 games, swatting 25 home runs and batting .280. He demonstrated that he was a wise investment and was named *The Sporting News* comeback player of the year for the American League. Veeck also made good on his hospital-bed pledge.

"At the end of the 1977 season, after having a big year, there was a note in my locker that said come up to the offices and see Bill Veeck," Soderholm said. "I went up to the office and he offered me a two-year contract at something like $150,000 a year, and I signed it immediately."

Soderholm wrote a cute poem about the 1977 season that read (on Zisk): "All of Richie's homers came from his mighty thunder thighs." (On Gamble:) "To think a man with Bozo hair could hit the ball so far / Thirty-one homers wasn't too bad for a man we named Radar." (On Chet Lemon:) "Batting seventh, we had a Lemon, so we called him Juice / He flagged 'em down in center field and kept the team so loose."

And about the final finish: "The season went by too quickly and many of us cried in our beer / The winter will pass by slowly as we await a better New Year. / We'll lose some players in the free-agent draft and some will be traded away / But there will always be a new hero who will take us to a pennant some day."

REFLECTIONS ON BASEBALL

Alas, for the White Sox and their fans, the conclusions drawn by Soderholm in the poem did not pan out exactly as he envisioned. The Sox did lose players to free agency, but did not acquire adequate replacements. Heroes were harder to come by in 1978 than they were in 1977 and it took decades before the Sox again claimed an American League pennant.

"I signed and the team fell apart," Soderholm said of the next season. "It was tough to go from that kind of great year, with the fans all hyped up and having an exciting year, to the next year when we couldn't seem to beat the Girl Scouts. It was a tough letdown. It really was. Boy, winning again I think is the toughest thing in sports. That's why I admire Tiger Woods and Michael Jordan and those kind of athletes. A lot of athletes get to the top and have that moment and time with the win and the glory and all of that stuff, but to maintain the level of intensity, to repeat over and over and over is the most difficult thing in all of sports."

Soderholm concluded a nine-year Major League career in 1980 and then operated successful private businesses in the Chicago area. One is called Front Row Tickets. For years Soderholm had groups of season tickets for both the White Sox and the Cubs. His heart was with the White Sox, but the Cubs constant sellouts were better for business. Asked if he still follows the dietary principles that helped him so much long ago, Soderholm said, "Hell, no." Fruits and vegetables are second string on the menu these days.

"I'm almost 60 years old," Soderholm said. "I want to play golf and enjoy my life. Candy bars? No problem."

Soderholm said he gets teased by people who have known him for a long time and read his conditioning book.

"It didn't sell too much," he said, "but it sold in some ballparks. To this day people come up and say, 'Oh, I had your book. Oh, god, look at you. Gee. You wrote a book on conditioning and now you weigh 250 pounds?' The way I look now I have to keep my love tank full, you know?"

Soderholm has pictures that include him in a White Sox uniform hanging out with Zisk or Gamble or other teammates and when he looks at them, he thinks, "God, I was once a professional athlete. It's hard to believe. I can barely walk around a golf course now. Too bad the body kind of wears out like a car. It just wears out on you after a while.

"But you know, I've had nothing less than a fabulous life," Soderholm said.

CHAPTER 16

LUKE APPLING

Lucas Benjamin "Luke" Appling was born in North Carolina in 1907, but he was closer to the red clay of Georgia. His family moved to Atlanta when he was still a child. Appling attended Oglethorpe College in the 1920s and he worked as a waiter in the dormitories as a freshman. Much later, Appling joked about the experience, saying he never broke a dish, which he knew was unbelievable for White Sox fans to imagine, given all the errors he made early in his career at shortstop. Besides being a superb baseball player, Appling had the goods as a halfback for Oglethorpe, too. He was a participant in underdog Oglethorpe's 13-7 historic upset of Georgia.

"Georgia just underestimated us," Appling said several years later. "It really should have beaten us."

By the end of his sophomore year, at Oglethorpe's athletic break-up dinner, Appling told his baseball coach he had been scouted by the Brooklyn Dodgers and was thinking of signing. When the coach expressed surprise that Appling thought he was ready for the majors, Appling said maybe he should try to set his sights on playing for the Southern League's Atlanta Crackers first.

Appling played the rest of the season for Atlanta and batted .326. White Sox officials saw him and purchased his contract. They liked him so much that they moved Appling into the lineup for six games before the end of the 1930 season and, as he always seemed able to do wherever he pulled on a uniform, Appling hit more than .300. Appling remained tied to the organization until after World War II.

Appling could hit better than he could field. He said he took some abuse from home fans for the way he bobbled grounders or threw them away in 1930, 1931, and 1932, when he sometimes was inserted into games at third base and second, as well as short. Besides his nerve-wracking juggling act in the field at first—he improved his glove prowess over the years—Appling established himself as perhaps the best foul-ball-hitting batter in baseball history. It is a compliment to call a hitter a batter with a good eye. No hitter was more patient or more precise. Appling could even direct foul balls into a certain area of the park.

One story goes that for White Sox games, Appling was trying to obtain free tickets for friends from Georgia, but when he made his request to the team secretary he was waved off because the man was too busy. Appling bought the tickets himself. When he got to thinking about it in the dugout, Appling became indignant at the brush-off. He told his teammates that he would make someone pay, though it was not clear if he was kidding or serious. During the game, roughly two dozen baseballs that Appling fouled off became fan souvenirs. The estimated cost was $30, about the cost of the tickets.

Another time, Appling was angered by a peanut vendor in the stands for making fun of a play on the field. He promptly fouled a pitch off that hit the seller in the head. Other times, Appling purposely tried to exhaust a team's ace by forcing him to throw extra pitches.

THE SETTING

Appling played in 130 games during the 1932 season, hitting .274 and getting some seasoning on the job, but broke out with a 151-game, .322 campaign in 1933. The guy could flat out hit. Most shortstops in the majors who were Appling contemporaries were glove men first and hitters second. One who approached Appling's statistics was Joe Cronin, also future president of the American

League, who hit .302 lifetime. Time and again, Appling was asked to explain his foul-ball hitting ability as a weapon against pitchers.

"Sooner or later the guy out there is bound to make a mistake and give me the pitch I want to hit," Appling said once.

Each year, Appling improved as a hitter. He did not boast about that talent, but he did brood about making errors. Finally, manager Jimmie Dykes took Appling aside and told him he had to play with more confidence and that he had to relax. Something clicked. Even in later years he sometimes felt his best hitting days were marred by a miscue in the field. Hitting was definitely what Appling knew best.

At the very end of his career in 1950, Appling was asked to reminisce about what he thought was his best game of all. He never made the World Series with the White Sox and there were no playoffs during his career, so Appling had to fish for a favorite individual performance. He explained his feelings about his best day to writer John C. Hoffman, and under the title "My Greatest Game," it was printed in *Baseball Digest*.

THE GAME OF MY LIFE
BY LUKE APPLING

CHICAGO WHITE SOX VS. ST. LOUIS BROWNS, AUGUST 5, 1933

I suppose a guy can't be around so long and not have a few good days. The game I think I'll always have to regard as my greatest was the one we played August 5, 1933, in St. Louis.

There are four things I'll remember most about that game. One was that I made five hits—three doubles and two singles—against the Browns. Another was that it was terribly hot. A third was that I will always believe I should have been credited with a sixth hit my last time at bat. And finally, Bump Hadley had been riding me pretty hard about not being able to hit to left field.

For a while in that game, it looked as if he were right. He kept throwing pitches outside so I'd hit to right field. He was not too much perturbed in the first inning when I hit a line drive over first base for my first double. I got my second double in the fourth inning and of course it went to right field. Jackie Hayes singled and we got our second run of the game. As I rounded third, Hadley gave me the works. "You couldn't throw a ball to left field."

I just laughed and told him I was going to pull his next pitch into left field. I was up again in the fifth inning and this time I singled, but again it went to right field. It was a high pitch outside and I guess I was lucky at that, but there were other hits by Mule Haas, Earl Webb, Jimmie Dykes and Charlie Berry and we scored four runs to lead the Browns, 6-5. When he saw my single going into right field, Bump yelled, "That's where you always hit them."

I made up my mind I was going to hit one to left field if it took all summer. So the next time up in the sixth inning, I doubled through short for my third double. Bump had been taking such a beating that I didn't have the heart to kid him about my hit to left field.

Well, they took him out of the game and I wasn't up again until the ninth inning. This time I hit a slow roller down the third-base line. Lynn Storti came in fast for the ball, made a grab for it, but I was on first before he could pick it up. I thought for sure it would be scored a hit and it made me feel pretty good to think I had made six hits in one game. But that night when I looked at the box score in the paper I saw where I had been credited with five hits. That didn't spoil it for me. Five hits is enough for anybody in one game.

GAME RESULTS

The White Sox actually lost, 10-9, to the Browns in the bottom of the 12th inning, and yes, Storti was given an error on the slow grounder. It seemed as if Hadley would have had enough to worry about with Appling batting safely every time without taking time out from his pitching concentration to taunt the hitter. Not that either team was within hailing distance of the pennant—the White Sox finished 16 games under .500 in 1933 and the Browns finished 41 games under .500. They did have enough time to chat for their own amusement.

The 1933 season represented Appling's first full .300 season at the plate, but by 1936 he was leading the league with a boggling .388 mark. Appling became an exemplary hitter and seemingly could hit anywhere at any time. Still, when asked to explain his batting championship, he chose the self-effacing phrase, "I don't know, except that I was just plain lucky."

A hitter has to be lucky enough for all nine fielders to fall down every time he comes to bat in order to hit .388, so there was more to it than that. Others spoke for him: Eddie Lopat, one of the mound mainstays for the New York Yankees in the 1940s and '50s, admired Appling's swings. "As a hitting shortstop, there was no one in his class," Lopat said.

When Appling's name was mentioned around the league, players nodded sagely, acknowledging readily that he was a dangerous hitter. Whenever they saw such an exhibition of Appling crushing foul balls into the seats, they were reminded of his bat control. But the other characteristic that always had the White Sox and sportswriters talking was his moaning and groaning about health problems. His nickname was "Old Aches and Pains." Sometimes Appling showed up at the ballpark complaining of illness. Sometimes he complained of fatigue. Sometimes he worried about a bad back, a bad knee, a sore elbow. Neither Manager Dykes, who oversaw much of Appling's career, nor his teammates really knew when he was truly hurting.

"If he had all the things wrong with him that he complains about," Dykes said, "he wouldn't have lasted two years. He's built like a rock, you know, and I don't think there's ever been anything wrong with him. To hear him tell it, he's never been right."

Humorously, the headline on the magazine story in *Collier's* where Dykes was quoted read, "Indestructible Shortstop."

Pulitzer Prize-winning *New York Times* sports columnist Arthur Daley called Appling the "Indestructible Invalid," recounting instances when Appling complained of being barely able to walk in the clubhouse, of suffering from double vision, and announcing he had appendicitis. He also complained at other times of a sprained wrist and a broken leg. The subhead on that newspaper story read, "The Hitting Hypochondriac."

It turns out that Appling was always a better player than he felt.

REFLECTIONS ON BASEBALL

After Appling retired from active duty in 1950, he stayed in the game. He managed White Sox farm teams for four years and won a pennant with Indianapolis of the American Assocation. In addition, Appling coached for the Baltimore Orioles, Detroit Tigers, Kansas City Athletics, and even scouted for Oakland before the White Sox summoned him back to Comiskey Park to coach in 1969. He was still popular in the old town, so the announcement of Appling rejoining the team he starred for was received agreeably. Appling enjoyed the idea of a reunion, too.

"It's nice to be back home," Appling said. "Chicago has always seemed like home to me. I have some very good friends there and it will be good to see all my cronies again."

Appling coached with the Sox for two years and then joined the Braves—in his real home of Atlanta—serving as a hitting instructor from 1976 until his death. Appling died in the hospital in Cumming, Georgia, in 1991 while undergoing surgery after he was admitted for an aneurysm of the aorta. Appling, who entertained baseball audiences with his stories for decades was described by Braves manager Bobby Cox as someone who lived as happy a life as anyone he had ever seen. In all, Appling spent 60 years in baseball.

Long after he officially retired from the White Sox, Appling had one more on-field thrill left in his bat. When he was 75 years old, Appling agreed to suit up for the Crackerjack Oldtimers Baseball Classic game for the benefit of retired players at RFK Stadium in Washington, D.C. Appling, the still-active hitting instructor, was in the lineup and came up to the plate to face southpaw Warren Spahn, the winningest left-hander of all time. Much to Spahn's, Appling's, the players, and the spectators' surprise, Appling cracked a home run off Spahn.

Spahn, who was 62 at the time, teased Appling beforehand, saying he would have to throw hard to him because there were too many younger players in the American League lineup. When Spahn's delivery came up fat, Appling swung and sent the ball soaring. As Appling eased into a home-run trot, a big grin on his face, Spahn ran over and swatted him with his glove. Spahn said he was trying to get a fake fight going for the fans, but Appling was too happy to be bothered and just kept thanking him. Later, Appling's wife kissed Spahn on the cheek and said, "Luke's boys believe what he says now."

Appling said the response to the blow was overwhelming. He had been in the game for nearly 60 years, had won batting titles, but in his dotage he received more attention for that home run than for anything else he ever did.

"That home run," he marveled in the years before he died, "gets more attention than any homer, or even any hit, that I ever had. It's pretty amazing."

CHAPTER 17

MINNIE MINOSO

For his entire youth and until sometime after he reached the major leagues, the ballplayer best known as Minnie was called Orestes. Friends still use that given name. To this day, more than 50 years after sportswriters began calling him Minnie in print, Minoso says he has no idea where the name came from. Saturnino Orestes Armas Arieta Minoso was born in Havana, Cuba.

There is nothing meek about Minnie Minoso, who followed a bold track in life to become a success. Raised in Cuban sugar-cane country outside of Havana, Minoso's early life was marked by deprivation. His parents divorced when he was eight and he lived in poverty in a home that had no electricity. His mother died when he was 10 and relatives took care of him in El Perico for a time. In his early teens, Minoso said he was milking cows and playing baseball whenever he could.

Although the *Baseball Enclyclopedia* lists Minoso's birth date as 1922, he insists he was born in 1925. He said sportswriters got it wrong.

"The newspaper writers never believed any player who was black and who came from South America," Minoso said. "I don't know why, but they said, 'No, he looks like he's older.' I don't care. I'm here."

After a couple of parentless years in the countryside, Minoso joined two sisters in Havana. In the city, he worked in a cigar factory and a candy factory, but he also polished his baseball. Minoso was old enough to see former Negro Leagues great Martin Dihigo play. Dihigo was likely the greatest Latin player of his era before the color barrier was broken in the majors. Although his main achievements would be logged in the outfield, Minoso was first a pitcher. That drew him even closer to Dihigo, who both pitched and played the field.

When he realized he was a good player, Minoso aspired to reach the top levels of play in the winter Latin American Leagues. As a dark-skinned Cuban, he never for a moment thought he would play in the United States for a team like the Chicago White Sox. In his mind, those doors were closed.

"There was no dream to play in the big leagues," he said. "That's the way things were then."

Yet the poor boy from the rural territory developed a parallel dream. He decided he would play in the U.S. after all, but in the Negro Leagues. Minoso's first language was Spanish and he knew little English when he joined the New York Cubans in 1945 at age 18. Minoso's combination of speed on the base paths, a big stick, a flamboyant style, and his friendly demeanor, made him an attractive catch for a Major League team once he matured with the Cubans. He starred in the Pacific Coast League and soon-to-be White Sox manager Paul Richards saw him there and mentally filed away his name. Minoso broke into the majors with Cleveland, playing nine games in 1949. He got a second chance with the Indians, briefly, in 1951, but was traded to the White Sox less than a month into the season.

"Paul Richards, he was the guy who wanted me," Minoso said. "And Frank Lane traded for me."

Although the trade was one of the most important and beneficial milestones in his life, Minoso didn't view it that way at the time. He felt betrayed by the Indians. He loved the organization and was close to Satchel Paige and Luke Easter, other black players who were in the forefront of American League integration. The Indians under Bill Veeck's ownership opened their clubhouse doors to black ballplayers almost as quickly as the Brooklyn Dodgers. Minoso's break-in time with the Indians marked his introduction to Veeck and was the start of a lifelong friendship.

When Minoso was shipped out of Cleveland, though, he felt he was losing all of his friends.

"I didn't want to leave the team I was with before Chicago," Minoso said. "I didn't know how to speak English and being with Luke Easter and Satchel Paige, I felt like they were kids I grew up with."

Minoso was in the middle of a hot streak at the plate against the St. Louis Browns when he was summoned to speak to Indians manager Al Lopez. He thought Lopez was going to compliment his fine play.

"I think he's going to say, 'Minnie, good going,'" Minoso recalled. "But he said, 'You've been traded to Chicago.' Just like that."

Minoso was crushed. He fled to his hotel room, put on some of his favorite music, and just sat there, gloomy and depressed.

"When they told me I was leaving, I felt my whole life was ending," Minoso said. After a while, there was a knock on the door. Teammate Ray Boone (whose son Bob and grandsons Aaron and Bret also became big leaguers) sought to comfort Minoso. His kind and encouraging words have stayed with Minoso forever.

"He said, 'Look, Minnie, I know how you feel, but it's good for you,'" Minoso recalled. "'You're a good ballplayer and it will be good for you. You're going to be OK.'"

There was also some more sinister discussion at the time that the Indians were moving too fast with integration and had too many black players on the team. Minoso said he always stayed in the black section of cities when the team traveled. He heard "one of the bosses" say the Indians had to trade a black player away because they had too many. Minoso said he asked general manager Hank Greenberg about that, but was told, "Minnie, that's not the reason." Minoso was headed to a new city and a new team. He was off to play for the Chicago White Sox, a club that had no other black players on its Major League roster.

THE SETTING

Baseball's greatest shame was the unwritten but well-supported and strongly enforced rule keeping dark-skinned men out of the Major Leagues for the first 47 years of the 20th century.

Dodgers general manager Branch Rickey spearheaded breaking the color barrier when he signed Jackie Robinson and brought him to Brooklyn in 1947. Rickey wanted to tap the new vein of talent previously consigned to the Negro Leagues. He wanted to win. He wanted to make money. But he also wanted societal change. Rickey did not want Robinson to be a solo act. He signed other black players quickly, too. Although less publicized in comparison to Robinson's breakthrough in the National League, Roy Campanella and Don Newcombe also integrated various minor leagues on their way up the promotion ladder.

For all the attention placed on Robinson as a pioneer, Veeck and the Indians were not far behind in integrating the Indians. Veeck signed Larry Doby and brought him to the majors a scant three months after Robinson. And as Veeck demonstrated by signing 42-year-old Satchel Paige, who played a key role in the Indians' World Series triumph, he was open to bringing aboard any player he thought would help. This spate of activity rubbed off on other big-league teams in varying degrees. But there were extra challenges for black Latino players who were not as adept at speaking English.

The White Sox had neither charged forward in the first wave of integration nor held back when a player became available who could help them win. That player was Minnie Minoso. When he was traded to Chicago, he became the first black player in White Sox history. When he started against the Yankees in 1951, he became the first black man to play in a Major-League game for the White Sox.

THE GAME OF MY LIFE
BY MINNIE MINOSO

CHICAGO WHITE SOX VS. NEW YORK YANKEES, MAY 1, 1951

The most important game of my life was May 1, 1951. I have a good memory and I always remember that date. I thank God for keeping my mind so clear. I never forget the good things. We were playing the Yankees and their pitcher was Vic Raschi. Eddie Robinson came up to me in the dugout and said, "Minoso, do you know this pitcher?" I said I had never faced him. He told me that he had a good fastball, a good curveball, and a good slider. So I went up to the plate my first time and I said I'm going to swing three times. I hit a long one that went 439 feet into the White Sox bullpen and the umpire signaled home run. I had the pleasure of hitting a home run before Mickey Mantle did in his career.

I made a good impression on the fans. White Sox fans always liked me after that. I never heard any boos. Never. Since that opening day, nobody ever booed. I was in love with everyone. I gave them my best and they gave me their hearts. The people looked at me like a good person.

Mr. Jackie and Mr. Branch Rickey opened the door to us. I don't ever look at race. I don't care for color, position, nationality, beauty, or ugliness. I knew about racism before I came from Cuba and that they say, "You're not supposed to be there." They have separate things and they don't let you eat there.

I am the first black player for the White Sox, but it had to be somebody. It is a good thing, but I am not a special person because of that. I paid my price, just like Jackie.

GAME RESULTS

The White Sox lost Minoso's debut, 8-3, and he made a costly error in the game that was a counterbalance to his home run. It was also the game when Mantle hit the first of his 536 career homers. But it was the beginning of something exciting for Minoso and the Sox. Minoso injected fresh life into the lineup, hitting 14 triples, 10 home runs, driving in 74 runs, batting .324, and stealing 31 bases. He was chosen American League rookie of the year and the fans were energized when he came to the plate or got on base.

"I've got the trophy at home," Minoso said.

Minoso became a seven-time All-Star outfielder. His arrival marked the beginning of the 1950s era of White Sox baseball, characterized by daring on the bases, scoring runs on small ball, and a team that could contend for the pennant. The phrase "Go-Go White Sox" was coined.

"I'm the one," Minoso said. "The fans yelled, 'Go, go, Minnie. Minnie, go.' I go when I think it is right. They could have got me out all of the time."

Minoso was a terrific all-around player. He could hit and hit with power and he shook up pitchers when he got on base because they couldn't predict whether he would go-go or not.

"Minnie was a tremendous ballplayer," former pitching teammate Billy Pierce said. "He had a lot of hustle. He would never want to give up. He could hit the long ball, knock in some runs, and run the bases well. He could go first to third with no effort."

Minoso was a staple of the White Sox' rejuvenated offense through the 1957 season as the team improved steadily and gave the Yankees some of their roughest challenges of the decade. However, when Al Lopez came over from the Indians to manage the Sox, Minoso was traded for a second time, back to the Indians. Minoso thinks it's more than coincidental that Lopez traded him twice, believing that he just didn't like him. When Bill Veeck became owner of the White Sox, he obtained Minoso again. The relationship between the two men grew closer over the years and when Veeck died, Minoso wore his White Sox uniform to the funeral. Everyone understood.

REFLECTIONS ON BASEBALL

Minoso retired from the majors in 1964 with a .298 lifetime average and if he had stayed retired and out of the limelight, he would be remembered fondly as a very able ballplayer. However, Minoso stayed active, playing, coaching, and managing in Mexico, and when Veeck bought the White Sox for a second time in the 1970s, he stunned the media at a press conference by introducing Minoso as his newest player. Courtesy of the new designated hitter rule which enabled him to join the lineup without playing in the field, at age 51 in 1976, Minoso appeared in three games and went one-for-eight.

That, everyone assumed, was that. But in 1980, Minoso was activated for two games, making him a rare five-decade player. An attempt to activate Minoso to become a six-decade player at first fizzled in the 1990s when the commissioner's office refused to sanction the move. Mike Veeck, Bill's son, stepped up and gave Minoso the chance to ride again in 1993 with the St. Paul Saints, an independent league team not under the jurisdiction of organized baseball. Likewise, in 2003 Minoso took his final cuts with the Saints in a game against Gary in the Northern League.

Hitting live pitches in seven different decades is a record unlikely to be matched. Although the cache is somewhat of a gimmick, many fans think it's a great accomplishment, and Minoso is proud that he was able to do it. When the White Sox won the 2005 World Series, they included Minoso in the list of longtime team associates given a championship ring. But he also wears a companion ring that commemorates his status as a seven-decade player.

"I think God gave me so much," Minoso said.

Minoso attends White Sox games whenever he can, regularly gets mail seeking autographs, and makes a couple of appearances each week representing the team in public. He particularly enjoys putting on his uniform and talking with school children.

"I show those youngsters that anything is possible," he said.

Many argue that Minoso should be in the Baseball Hall of Fame, but he said he does not dwell on that. He is a member of Mexico's baseball Hall of Fame and is happy the way his life turned out. Sometimes he reflects on how far he came from poverty in Cuba to being recognized on the streets of Chicago where people call his name and wave to him.

"I've come from nowhere," Minoso said. "Sometimes I lie down at my house and cry; tears come from my eyes. I don't know how to thank the people. In Chicago, everybody knows me. The people give me love. I don't have the words to say how much it means to me. Did I deserve this? Everyone treats me like I am part of their family. It seems like a dream."

CHAPTER 18

WILBUR WOOD

Wilbur Wood grew up in the Boston suburb of Belmont as a Red Sox fan. He started playing baseball in Little League and followed the typical youth track through high school, playing Babe Ruth-level ball, playing for his school and the American Legion. In high school, where he was nicknamed "Butch" by some and "Woody" by others, he was quarterback of the football team.

Wood played before the Major League draft, when teams still employed squadrons of full- and part-time scouts to scour sandlots.

"That's how it all began for me," Wood said. "At the time, all the ball clubs had scouts in local areas. That's what you were always dreaming about, that the Red Sox would find you."

Wood had good potential and several teams were interested in him. Although his heart was with the Red Sox, he said the negotiations were all business, with a limited amount of sentiment. However, Tommy Brewer, a solid Red Sox pitcher of the late 1950s and '60s, was renting a house in Belmont next door to good friends of the Wood family and he invited Wood to his house for a talk.

"He was nice enough to ask me if I would like to come over and sit down, and we did," Wood said. "He was very enlightening. Not just about the Red Sox. He explained how a lot of things worked and how much money you would get playing in the minors."

The standard minor-league pay was $400 a month, Wood said, and he was being offered $1,000 a month in addition to a bonus to sign.

"Money-wise, I was king of the hill in the minors," Wood said.

Wood came close to giving up baseball altogether, however. His father played baseball and basketball at Boston University and Wood nearly went to college on a hockey scholarship. He was a defenseman tempted to choose that direction for his sporting career, and later in life he was still an avid pick-up game participant. Wood was just 19 when he first pulled on a Red Sox uniform for a real game in 1961— he appeared in six games, debuting on the road.

"It was a great thrill," he said. "It was absolutely something special. Next home stand I pitched at Fenway. It was a good feeling every time you put a big-league uniform on. Obviously, I wasn't very successful."

Wood's record was 0-0 in 1961 and 0-0 in 1962. He was 0-5 in 1963 and during the 1964 season he was shipped to the Pittsburgh Pirates. Wood's fastball wasn't as fast as it had seemed and it didn't seem as if he would ever break through with Boston.

"The first game I won was when I was in Pittsburgh," Wood said.

Being puckish and experimental as far back as a 12-year-old Little Leaguer, Wood first dabbled in trying to throw a knuckleball—for fun. It was not part of his pitching repertoire. Then, as now, scouts are most smitten with a pitcher's velocity, and knucklers can float up to the plate at 68 mph. In spring training of 1966, Wood was cut from the Pirates and assigned to the team's AAA Columbus team of the International League. By that time, Wood had experienced five Major-League call-ups with the Red Sox and Pirates and had been unable to stick and produce.

Wood felt the end of his baseball career was near. He had worked as an apprentice plumber for his father-in-law and felt that might have been a way to go. That night over dinner, as they pondered their future, Wilbur and his wife, Sandra, discussed what else he could do to hang on. He said he had never poured all of his energy into making the knuckleball his key pitch. He decided to give that a try.

Everything came together for Wood that summer in Columbus. He led the league in innings and won 14 games. A White Sox scout saw him throw and convinced management to buy his contract.

By 1967, when Wood appeared in 51 games for the White Sox as a reliever, he was beginning to master the tricky pitch. Better than anything for Wood's development, the White Sox already had one of the greatest knuckleball pitchers of all time on the roster. Hoyt Wilhelm was the pre-eminent practitioner of the pitch during the 1960s and for Wood it was like having a personal coach sitting next to him in the bullpen. Wood is forever grateful for the advice and encouragement imparted to him by the late Wilhelm.

"He taught me more about the knuckleball in one day than I ever knew before," Wood mentioned in 1971. "He took me aside in spring training and in five minutes he showed me why the knuckleball was good and why it was bad. I never can thank him enough."

In 1968, almost as if he had been in hibernation, Wood exploded on the American League scene with a record 88 appearances while collecting 13 wins and 16 saves in relief. He was the talk of the league, especially because the knuckler was so hard to hit. Batters trained to swing at 90-mph fastballs were continously fooled by the fluttering knuckler that seemed to defy gravity. Often they looked silly on a swing, missing the ball by a foot.

In 1970, the White Sox hired Chuck Tanner as manager and Johnny Sain as pitching coach. Tanner was a player's manager with a flexible nature, willing to try different things. Sain is hailed as perhaps the greatest pitching coach of all time. They concluded that Wood was probably the best hurler on the team and decided that he should be starting. Wood was moved into the rotation for the 1971 season and magic ensued.

Over the next four seasons, Wood won 22, 24, 24, and 20 games for the White Sox. The knuckler put almost no stress on his pitching arm and he repeatedly made starts on two days' rest. The left-hander said his arm never tired and that if Tanner would let him he would start both games of a doubleheader in the same day. Tanner did not welcome Wood's entreaties with open arms, more or less laughing off

Wood's lobbying. However, there came a day—or two days—when circumstances dictated that the best chance the White Sox had to win two games was to use Wood on very short rest.

THE SETTING

Wood was a unique weapon. No one else had a pitcher who could start on short rest, go long innings, and remain unaffected. A review of Wood's statistics between 1971 and 1974 amounts to a post-1920 aberration. In 1973, Wood won 24 games, but he lost 20, the last time any pitcher hit the 20s on both sides of the ledger. During those four years, Wood never threw less than 320⅓ innings. In 1972 he pitched 376 ⅔ inningsæalmost two season's worth for many starters of 2008. Also that year, Wood started 49 games. The last time someone on the White Sox did so was in 1908, when Big Ed Walsh, a man clearly of another era, started with the same frequency. Current-day rotation pitchers usually start around 32 games.

It was as if Wood were making up for lost time. Those 0-0 years in the majors and those struggles in the minors were in the past, but Wood kept telling anyone who would listen that he could pitch just about every day because his arm never got tired. Why? The knuckler. It didn't stress those arm muscles. Wood bet his livelihood on the unpredictable pitch. For him the fastball became his change of pace.

"Hoyt convinced me that if the knuckler was my best pitch, I'd succeed only if I threw it at least 90 percent of the time," Wood said.

It was counter to all baseball philosophy to use your best starting pitcher on short rest so often. However, a pitcher with a rubber arm like Wood could relieve and start and pitch, often and long. It came to pass that during one stretch of the 1973 season Tanner called on Wood twice rather quickly, and the results pleased Wood more than any other game he pitched.

THE GAMES OF MY LIFE
BY WILBUR WOOD

CHICAGO WHITE SOX VS. CLEVELAND INDIANS,
MAY 26 AND MAY 28, 1973

Probably one of the biggest things I enjoyed was a situation where one game went into extra innings and I pitched, then the game after that I was scheduled to start. They were against the Indians. The first game was an extra-inning night game and there was a curfew in Chicago where you couldn't start a game after 1 a.m. or what have you. So we had a suspended game. The game lasted 21 innings and I pitched the last five innings and got the win. The time of the game was more than six hours and a few guys had nine official at-bats. Dick Allen hit a home run in the bottom of the last inning to win the game.

A day later, it was my turn to pitch and I went out and threw a complete-game shutout, a four-hitter. So I ended up pitching 14 innings. I gave up one run in the first game, but we tied it again. It wasn't like closers today where they come in and pitch a third of an inning here and a third of an inning there and get two wins. It didn't work like that.

When Chuck Tanner brought me into the first game, you figure it's only going to go one or two innings and it's going to end up one way or the other. It just so happened that it went on and on. He asked me if I wanted to go back out for the start and I said I did. Now there's a federal case about pitch counts if anybody throws 110 pitches. If they had agents at the time, which we didn't really have, and I did what I did, the agent would be calling the general manager and yelling, "What are you doing? You're ruining my client!"

GAME RESULTS

The White Sox defeated the Indians, 6-3, in the first game. Wood struck out five batters, but gave up a run in the top of the 21st before Chicago rallied behind Allen's three-run homer. The Sox starter, who had plenty of time to shower, dress, and drive home, was Stan

Bahnsen, and he pitched a stalwart 13 innings that game. The loser in that encounter was Ed Farmer, now a White Sox radio broadcaster.

Wood was in total command the second game against the Indians, surrendering just four hits and striking out four. The game ended in a swift 1 hour and 57 minutes. Wood was at the peak of his prowess at that time, pitching often and well. The White Sox, though, were a so-so team, finishing 77-83 in 1973. During his high times of the early 1970s, Wood was the object of much media attention, mostly writers wondering how he pitched so often without becoming fatigued like his colleagues.

"For quite a few years I was pitching twice a week," he said. "We always had a doubleheader on Sundays, and then had Mondays off. I was pitching Wednesday and Sunday. I did that for about two and a half years."

It seemed as if Wood would be able to pitch forever. He wasn't going to wear out his arm. But his luck didn't hold out as long as that left arm. Wood eventually did get a chance to start both games of a doubleheader, but it didn't work out—he lost both games.

His real problems began during a May, 1976 game against the Detroit Tigers. Ron LeFlore struck a wicked line drive that fractured Wood's left kneecap. Pitchers are forever being forced to the sidelines by torn rotator cuffs, sore elbows, and arm woes of every conceivable type.

Wood's season ended abruptly. He appeared in only 24 games the next year and finished his career with a 10-10 mark in 1978. His wounded knee did him in; otherwise Wood might have pitched another 10 years.

REFLECTIONS ON BASEBALL

Always an active fisherman, Wood, who enjoyed surf fishing for striped bass and blue fish, owned a fish market for about four and a half years after he retired.

"It was a lot of fun," Wood said. "But everything changes and it became harder to drive to the beaches. You couldn't get access to those places."

Wood tried a new profession. A friend of a friend connnected him with a company called Geneva Pharmaceuticals and he worked in the hospital division covering the New England area for about a dozen years. Then he became a national account manager for Carolina Products.

Periodically, Wood appears at sports memorabilia shows and signs autographs. He follows the progress of his hometown Boston Red Sox and his longtime employer, the Chicago White Sox, and he takes a particular interest in any pitcher who throws the knuckler. The most prominent knuckleballer in the majors these days, according to Wood, is Boston's Tim Wakefield. Knuckleball pitchers have spells where the knuckler controls them as much as they control the pitch. And because of that uncertainty, managers, especially those of the insecure variety, get nervous when they bring in a knuckleballer.

"Not every catcher can catch the knuckler," Wood said. "And a lot of pitchers can't really throw it. The thing of it is, everyone who wants to start throwing a knuckleball decides to do that after they've hurt their arm. They didn't start young. But if your arm is bothering you, you can't throw it."

Wood doesn't think there will ever be a large number of pitchers counting on the knuckleball. It will always be the secret weapon of the rare pitcher who has patience, the right temperament, and an inability to throw a fastball more than 90 mph. For those rare few, the knuckler will always be a savior.

CHAPTER 19

CHUCK TANNER

Charles William "Chuck" Tanner was a good athlete as a youth in New Castle, Pennsylvania. He participated in football, basketball, track, and baseball.

"I played sports all my life," Tanner said. "That was all I wanted to do."

He loved baseball the most and took advantage of any type of organized team, even though his career predates Little League. He played American Legion ball in Pennsylvania and was a high school star. Here the then-Boston Braves spotted Tanner. He was 17 going on 18. Before he knew it he was playing baseball for money (a small amount of money) in Class D in Owensboro, Kentucky. He was an immediate success, batting .330.

In the late 1940s and early 1950s, minor league baseball dominated the American landscape. And Major League teams, most of them following the Branch Rickey farm system model established with the St. Louis Cardinals, were affiliated with many teams from Class D right up the line to Class A, AA, and AAA.

"They moved me up to Class C and I hit .360," Tanner said. "I skipped B and went to A. There was no room upstairs because they already had so many players."

Tanner worked his way through the minors and made his Major League debut with the Braves on April 12, 1955, though by that time they had moved to Milwaukee. After a year-long wait, at 26 Tanner smacked a home run on the first pitch of his first big-league at-bat off Gerry Staley. He batted .247 in 97 games, but never displayed the hitting stroke in the majors that he had shown in the minors. He settled into a life as a career back-up, valuable to teams, but with not enough pop in his bat to ever become more than a periodic regular. Still, after making it to the Show, Tanner established a secondary goal—staying in the majors for five years and earning a pension. He accomplished that, too.

Long ago, Tanner said that when he was a 17-year-old leaving home to play professional baseball, he felt like if he played one game in the majors his life would be complete. He ended up playing 396. But then he put a new goal on his life list—to manage a Major League team.

Tanner, who thought he had seen the entire minor-league world during nine seasons of below-the-radar play, returned to the minors to establish managerial credentials. He won manager of the year awards in the Texas League and the Pacific Coast League with Hawaii before being getting his big break with the White Sox with about a month to go in the 1970 season. The White Sox were in a tailspin, about to finish a 56-win season, and Tanner managed only the last 16 games of the disaster, winning three. His main function was to evaluate the talent and see who should be retained and who replaced.

"I just let them play and I observed and analyzed them," Tanner said. "I told them the only thing I'm going to do is change pitching."

That was just a warm-up. For a new season, a lot was going to change.

THE SETTING

Chuck Tanner was the third man to hold the title of Chicago White Sox manager during the 1970 season. Don Gutteridge's two-season tenure was cut short. Third base coach Billy Adair was interim manager for 10 days and then Tanner took over September 13. The team's record was 56-106. Between the end of the 1970 season and the start of the 1971 season there were a multitude of player shuf-flings. If your winning percentage is .346 and you finish 42 games out of first place you can't stand pat.

Among the players traded away were Gail Hopkins, Ken Berry, Jose Ortiz, local legend Luis Aparicio, Tommy McCraw, and Duane Josephson. Among the players arriving were Pat Kelly, Jay Johnstone, Tom Bradley, Dave Lemonds, Mike Andrews, Luis Alvarado, Bill Robinson, Rick Reichardt, Ed Stroud, Vincente Romo, and Tony Muser. For fans, it was almost as if you couldn't tell who the players were without a scorecard. Heck, the manager and coaches probably couldn't tell the players apart without a roster sheet in spring training.

At the same time that the White Sox slumped to the bottom of the American League, the Oakland Athletics were on the rise. A's owner Charlie Finley recognized the talent he had in place and was rightly confident his team was on the cusp of something big. Starting in 1971, the A's won five straight Western Division titles and won three straight World Series championships between 1972 and 1974.

All of that lay in the future. The White Sox were scheduled to open at Oakland in 1971 to play a doubleheader. Tanner said Finley used his influence on the schedule makers to begin the season that way.

"The reason he did that was because he figured the A's would be 2-0 since the White Sox had the worst record in baseball," Tanner said. "I don't know if he said it publicly, but I heard that—'We'll be 2-0.'"

THE GAME OF MY LIFE
BY CHUCK TANNER

CHICAGO WHITE SOX VS. OAKLAND ATHLETICS, APRIL 7, 1971

I was thinking that I had a different team than the year before, that we could come out and be 2-0. Tommy John started the first game and we came back and beat the A's in the late innings with a home run. I used Vincente Romo out of the bullpen to save the game.

Then we had the second game and we won easily. Nobody knew the A's were going to be a dynasty at that point, but we knew we beat a good team. I think we hurt Charlie Finley's feelings, too. People didn't even know who half the people on our team were. I had six kids I brought up from A ball, or somewhere in the minors.

The wins helped us in other ways, too. When the season started, nobody was talking about the White Sox. The organization hadn't even planned for that many people to come to the home opener. They never anticipated a crowd because they were 56-106.

They figured on maybe 10,000 or 12,000 people. I don't know if it was because we won that doubleheader or not, but we got people excited and we had a big crowd. By the fifth inning they had sold out of food. And we won that one, too. We were 3-0.

GAME RESULTS

Tanner, who made bigger and better memories leading the Pittsburgh Pirates to a World Series championship, looks back on the A's doubleheader fondly. He resented the idea that his team was being taken for granted. The final score of the opener was 6-5 White Sox, and the Sox beat future Hall of Famer Jim "Catfish" Hunter with two runs in the top of the seventh. The key blow was a home run by Bill Melton. The Sox won the second game, 12-4, and youngster Bart Johnson collected the win with a complete game. The A's starter that day was another future Hall of Famer, Rollie Fingers, who mostly made his living in relief. Jay Johnstone and Mike Andrews each went 3-for-4.

The home opener did pack 'em in, with a paid attendance of 43,253 present for the White Sox's 3-2 victory over the Minnesota Twins. Although Bradley pitched strongly for eight innings, Romo got the win in that game. The pre-season acquisitions were paying dividends in a hurry.

Tanner remembers a pivotal point in the season when he argued with upper management over bringing up veteran outfielder Mike Hershberger from the minors where he had rehabbed an injury.

Hershberger played 74 games for the White Sox that summer and hit .265, his last season in the big leagues. Tanner recalls Hershberger going on an immediate tear when he joined the big club.

"I never heard anything after that," Tanner said. "Hershberger did the job, solidified us, and that's why we finished third. I believe that move we made bringing him up was one of the big reasons."

The White Sox finished a so-so 79-83, but it was a 23-game improvement in the win column and the next year the team won 87 games and challenged Oakland. Fans started to care about what happened again and began believing that good things would happen. Owner John Allyn was pleased by the turnaround.

"Actually, John Allyn said we saved the franchise here in Chicago," Tanner said.

Tanner, who still lives near Dick Allen in Pennsylvania, always had a solid relationship with the player other teams shunned. Allen's reputation was of a hard-to-deal-with guy, but he and Tanner thrived together. Allen won the Most Valuable Player award as a White Sox and Tanner won games because Allen played so well.

"He grew up like 20 minutes from where I lived," Tanner said. "He goes out to my kid's farm. My boy Gary has a horse and he spends three or four hours with Gary. Dick raises horses. Dick Allen is one of the greatest players in the history of the White Sox."

REFLECTING ON BASEBALL

Tanner served as White Sox manager from 1970 to 1975 and felt the team was poised to win a pennant after the 87-win 1972 season. But during a time of changing baseball economics, when big salaries were being shelled out for the first crop of free agents, the club lagged behind and slipped backwards.

"I thought we had it going," Tanner said. "Then we weren't able to do a lot of things because we didn't have much money. Consequently, we'd make trades and get cash in return because we needed it. We did everything to keep the White Sox afloat. It wasn't enough. Mr. Allyn had to sell the club."

Tanner, who uttered the thought a decade later in an interview with the *Christian Science Monitor*, learned an important lesson early in his managing career. "There are three secrets to managing," he said. "The first secret is to have patience. The second is to be patient. And the third most important secret is patience."

Tanner and his brilliant pitching coach Johnny Sain ("The best ever," Tanner claimed) displayed patience and creativity with some of their top hurlers. Jim Kaat came to the White Sox in 1973 and spent a little more than two years with the team, winning 20 games twice. Sain and Tanner worked with Kaat to develop a new, quicker delivery and the change added years to his career. When Kaat, who pitched for 26 years and then became a broadcaster, wrote a book about his life in baseball, he called Tanner the best manager he ever played for. And to his face, he thanked Tanner for his help, praising him for extending his career.

It was also under the Tanner-Sain regime that Wilbur Wood, knuckleballer supreme, shifted from relief pitcher to starter.

"Fred Shaffer, one of the scouts, who was from my hometown," Tanner said, "said he had seen Wilbur pitch in AAA for the Pirates. He said he could be a good starter. I went to Wilbur and said, 'Do you want to make a lot of money?' He said, 'Yeah.' I said, 'I'm gonna start you.' I pitched him with two days' rest, three days' rest. He won 24 games. He pitched 370-something innings. If he hadn't gotten hit on the knee with that line drive I don't know how long he could have pitched. Easily until he was 50."

Soon after Tanner made the announcement about changing Wood's role, he was in old Comiskey Park's Bard's Room eating a sandwich and said the writers and announcers were standing around eating, drinking, and critiquing the move. The consensus was: how the heck can they start Wilbur Wood?

"There wasn't one guy who thought that was a good idea," Tanner said. "It was like, 'What is that young guy trying to do?' Now, when Wilbur won his 20th game, I was up there getting a sandwich and unanimously all of them said, 'Well, that was the right move to make. Everybody knows with that knuckleball he should have been a starter his whole career.' I just kind of smiled to myself."

Tanner later managed the Pirates to a World Series title and led the A's and Atlanta Braves before leaving the dugout in 1988. His son Bruce grew up to become a Major Leaguer, too, pitching in 10 games for the White Sox in 1985.

Tanner got involved with race horses, as part owner of a three-year-old named Majesty's Imp that he thought was of Kentucky Derby caliber. He joked that he wanted to be the first person to win a World Series and a Kentucky Derby. Always a horse fan, Tanner said he and Kaat bought a horse together in 1976 and it won its first race.

But Tanner never left baseball. After 60 years in the game, in the fall of 2007 he took on the job of senior advisor for baseball operations for the Pirates after serving as a Pennylvania-based scout for the Cleveland Indians. Tanner was already attending the 81 Pirates home games scouting for potential Indians trades.

"I go to all the games and I love it," Tanner said.

He laughed when it was suggested that his longevity might beat out Connie Mack, whose autobiography discussed his 66 years in baseball.

"Not quite," Tanner said.

In 1989, the year after the Braves fired him, Tanner acted as a front man for a group of anonymous wealthy investors who sought to buy a Major League team. They never got a deal.

As his first manager's job, the White Sox days remain memorable to Tanner. But more than that he appreciates the commitment of fans who had to put up with losing teams for so long and still stay in touch with him.

"I still get mail from them," Tanner said. "Those White Sox have great fans."

In a 1985 interview with the *Sporting News*, Tanner's unending enthusiasm for baseball came through. "The greatest feeling in the world is to win a Major League game," he said. "The second greatest feeling is to lose a Major League game."

Indeed, the most important thing for Chuck Tanner is that you get to play the game.

CHAPTER 20

ROLAND HEMOND

Born in 1929, Roland Hemond grew up in Central Falls, Rhode Island—a mill town near Pawtucket, currently the home of the Boston Red Sox AAA farm club. He said he saw the first game ever played in McCoy Stadium in 1942. His father, Ernest, was a bread salesman for more than 30 years. His mother, Antoinette, a seamstress, was from a suburb of Montreal, and for the first six years of his life, Hemond spoke mainly French. But he still became a baseball fan quickly.

"I saw my first big-league game in 1938," Hemond said. "Jimmie Foxx hit a home run. I was a die-hard Red Sox fan."

Hemond was also a passionate player, competing for the local Boys Club in what he described as Sunday leagues, and in American Legion and high school baseball. Hemond would have loved to play baseball as a career.

"I realized I didn't have the ability," he said, "and that my destiny would not be to be a big-league player. I was a little guy and just loved the game."

After Hemond graduated from high school he joined the Coast Guard and spent four years in that branch of the service. In 1951, while on leave, Hemond thought about a way to make a livelihood out of baseball and hopped a free Coast Guard flight to Florida to explore opportunities. He had a cousin named Ray Lague in the

Pittsburgh Pirates organization and he thought he would touch base and try to make some contacts. If that didn't work out, he thought he might try umpiring school, or Providence College, where he could major in journalism and become a sportswriter. Anything to stay close to the game.

Hemond arrived in Deland, only to discover that his timing was off, that the big club had put back the start of spring training for three days. He met a blind man named Leo McMahon, who had been wounded in World War I and operated a boarding house with one unrented room. Hemond took it, became friendly with the owners, and discovered that the blind man sang the national anthem at minor-league parks under the name "The Lucky Sergeant." He wrote Hemond a general letter of introduction to show to baseball officials and before the spring was out Hemond was making $28 a week working for the Boston Braves' Hartford Chiefs, a Class A affiliate. Hemond's job description was on the vague side. He was supposed to do whatever needed to be done around the ballpark.

"I would start the day by unlocking the ballpark," Hemond said.

Then he joined the trainer in tag-team sweeping and grandstand cleanup. Then he helped open the concession stands and sold tickets. A little bit of everything. Interns who take summer jobs with minor-league teams do much the same kind of work today.

"It's a good way to start," Hemond said, "because you can appreciate what everybody has to do. Then the manager said he couldn't afford me."

It looked like a short life in baseball for Hemond, but his phone rang 10 days later. He had an interview with Braves farm and scouting director John Mullen.

"He said he'd give me a two-week tryout," Hemond said. "I'm still in baseball 57 years later."

Ex-White Sox manager Chuck Tanner, who worked for years with Hemond once said, "He would give anyone an opportunity who loved the game and was willing to start at the bottom. He always had time for the little guy starting out, because he sold peanuts and popcorn."

Braves general manager John Quinn's 11-year-old daughter used to hang out in the office and drive the hired help like Hemond crazy by fooling around with the names on the team's minor league roster boards. After she grew up, Margo Quinn became Hemond's wife.

THE SETTING

Doing the little things well got Hemond noticed, and in the insular world of baseball management he earned a good reputation. Hemond worked up to assistant farm and scouting director of the Milwaukee Braves. He got his second big break as director of scouting systems and the farm teams of the Los Angeles Angels in 1961. He stayed with the Angels until joining the White Sox in 1971, first handling the functions of assistant general manager. In July of 1973, Hemond was promoted to general manager and he remained in that role through the 1985 season, wheeling and dealing for players, signing contracts, and as the dynamics of the sport changed, supervising the team's involvement in the free agent market, a task not unlike gambling on stocks.

Carlton Fisk, the Hall of Fame catcher, was the cornerstone of the Boston Red Sox, the signature player in the lineup, revered by New Englanders. He was also a veteran who broke into the majors in 1969, and when he became a free agent leading up to the 1981 season there was no way to tell how much longevity he had left. What no one, not Fisk, Hemond, nor any other baseball observer could know was that Fisk was going to turn out to be the sturdiest catcher of all time. At the time, Hemond just hoped the signing of Fisk would turn out well for the White Sox.

THE GAME OF MY LIFE
BY ROLAND HEMOND

CHICAGO WHITE SOX VS. BOSTON RED SOX, APRIL 10, 1981

Carlton Fisk became a free agent on a technicality because the Red Sox had been late sending him his contract for the following year. That made him a free agent and available to us. And then the very first game he was to play for us was in Boston. I actually said, "Gee, I wish he was playing someplace else." It was their opening day in Fenway Park and there was a lot of emotion and feeling because he was wearing a White Sox uniform and returning to Boston. There was a lot going on in the air. And I was born and raised as a Red Sox fan in Rhode Island.

Late in the game the Red Sox had Bob Stanley on the mound in relief and Fisk came up to the plate. It was the top of the eighth inning and Fisk hit a three-run homer off Stanley that turned out to be the winning runs.

My sister was with me and I gave her a big kiss when the ball left the park. I went down and kissed Linda Fisk, Carlton's wife, also. Carlton's son Casey was the bat boy to meet him at home plate. That was quite a moment. I'm not sure Carlton Fisk would classify it as one of his biggest games, but I thought it was pretty special.

GAME RESULTS

Fisk's three-run homer gave the White Sox a 3-2 lead in a game they won 5-3. Fisk had a fine day at the plate, going two-for-four with three RBIs and a run scored. More importantly for Hemond and the White Sox, Fisk taking up residence in the lineup seemed to signal the start of a new era for Chicago. In 1983, the White Sox won 99 games and romped to a first-place finish in the American League West, finishing 20 games ahead of Kansas City in the standings.

Four days later, after a two-game series in Boston, the White Sox played their home opener against the Milwaukee Brewers and Fisk made just as big a splash at Comiskey Park.

"He hit a home run—a grand slam—in the first inning off Pete Vuckovich," Hemond recalled.

Hemond has many good memories of the highlights from his days with the White Sox. Helping guide the White Sox to that West Division title in 1983—and the players who shared in it—also stands out in Hemond's memory. Tony La Russa was a young manager, and the team featured sluggers like Fisk, Harold Baines, Ron Kittle, and

Greg Luzinski. The Sox dominated their division, and winning the crown was just a matter of time once they built their lead, but when it actually happened it was still a shock.

"When we clinched the division in 1983, that was a great feeling," Hemond said. "It was closer for a long while, but we got hot and couldn't lose and Kansas City fell way behind. We had a substantial lead and I felt when we clinched it, it might not be as climactic as we'd like it to be. But when Harold Baines hit the fly ball to center for a sacrifice and Julio Cruz crossed the plate, it was bedlam. It was a great celebration, despite the fact that it was inevitable that we would win it. That was a big moment."

That season was commemorated by the song "Winning Ugly," mostly because the White Sox won any which way they could. Few remember how slowly the team started, struggling with a 12-13 record, but the Sox finished 33 games over .500 after the July All-Star break.

REFLECTIONS ON BASEBALL

Few things are forever in sports and not even Hemond's tenure operating the White Sox fit that description. Despite earning executive of the year honors in 1972 and 1983 with the White Sox, he was fired as general manager after the 1985 season. Hemond spent one year as special assistant to the chairman of the board and then, even though he was always closely identified with the White Sox, Hemond spent most of the next 15 years working for other baseball teams. In 1989 while with the Orioles, he was named executive of the year again.

In 2001, Hemond returned to the White Sox fold as an advisor to general manager Kenny Williams and stayed in that capacity until 2007 when he hooked up with the Arizona Diamondbacks for a second time, just in time for the Snakes to win their division and advance to the playoffs.

Hemond often said the White Sox were his favorite employers and that Chicago was his favorite town. He loves to talk baseball and, despite a lifetime of devotion to the sport, he never tires of it. He says he watches 200 games a year, but he watches those games with a more clinical eye than most fans. Hemond is always evaluating talent— can't help it. It's what he is supposed to do. If he sees a minor leaguer, a player in another country, or a player in another big-league uniform, his mind is taking pictures, trying to figure out if the player has long-term potential or instant potential if the club traded for him. A 2003 *Chicago Tribune* story attributed more than 150 trades to Hemond during his front-office career.

Hemond has played many additional roles in baseball, working with Team USA while squads were readying for the Pan American Games and the 2000 Summer Olympics, and working in the commissioner's office with Peter Ueberroth. Hemond, of course, also married into baseball. His wife Margo's father, John Quinn, was a three-decades baseball executive and her brother Bob Quinn was a Major League general manager. The Hemonds' sons have also both played roles in baseball.

Hemond's perpetually positive attitude, his accomplishments running teams, and his influence on many up-and-coming front office executives has been honored in several ways. He was presented the Branch Rickey Award by the Rotary Club of Denver in 2003 that goes to an individual in baseball who contributes unselfishly to his community and serves as a role model. In 2001, Hemond was recognized by minor league baseball for his contributions with the honor "King of Baseball." He has served as president of the Association of Professional Ballplayers of America, which helps former and present ballplayers in need, and he also helped found the Professional Baseball Scouts Foundation to provide aid to scouts.

Hemond is gray-haired and remains slender, but even well into his seventies, he never seems to run short of energy, especially if it means being on hand for important baseball moments. When the White Sox made their run through the playoffs and defeated the Houston Astros in four games in the 2005 World Series, Hemond was on staff in the front office and attended certain playoff games and all of the Series events. In the excitement of a third-game Sox victory, he even forgot about his own birthday.

"When Geoff Blum hit the home run it was after midnight," Hemond said. "It was a long game and when the ball left the park my wife turned to me and said, 'Happy birthday, Lovey.' She realized I was oblivious to the fact it was now my birthday. So we embraced. I was embarrassed to celebrate early because the other club still had to hit. Our children were calling on the cell phone wishing me happy birthday and they reminded me we could win another game the same day, which we did, and won the World Series. In some ways that day was the highlight of them all. Knowing the joy that a fan would derive from it, that's the reward you always wanted to accomplish. That gives personal happiness and satisfaction to Sox fans. It was incredible. It was the culmination of dreams. I was so happy for Sox fans, owner Jerry Reinsdorf, the whole organization. It was just unbelievable."

Maintaining his primary residence in Arizona gave Hemond a good base to see spring training, the fall instructional league, and Diamondbacks home games.

"It adds up to a lot of games I see," Hemond said. "I see baseball day in and day out."

Not that he ever tires of haunting ballparks, even after a half century-plus.

"Not at all," he said. "I love it."

CHAPTER 21

RON KITTLE

The love of the game in the Kittle household ran deep. Ron's father James was a huge baseball fan. He had ties to areas of Maryland and West Virginia and followed the Baltimore Orioles. He watched baseball on television and listened on the radio as Ron grew up in Gary, Indiana.

"He had the TV and the radio blaring all of the time," Kittle said. "So I kind of grew up watching. Brooks Robinson was my favorite player."

Kittle started playing baseball when he was very young, but didn't stick with one position. He played wherever a coach put him, from catcher to outfielder. Unlike many talented youngsters, though, he did not take to the mound.

"I only pitched one time in my whole life and it was probably the biggest mistake I've ever seen," Kittle said.

James Kittle was an iron worker who put in 12-hour days to feed a family with six kids, so he didn't have time to coach his son. Ron Kittle loved baseball so much that some days he put on his Little League uniform and walked 10 blocks to the field, just to watch other teams play. His parents didn't mind.

"They knew I loved baseball and they figured, 'We would rather have our son at the ballpark than doing something else,'" he said. "I would sit there and watch and chase foul balls and get a popsicle in return."

Kittle, who grew up to be 6-foot-4 and 220 pounds, started to emerge from the pack of kids when he was about 11 years old. His dad offered to pay him $5 for every home run he hit. Kittle hit a home run. Then another. And another. Soon the reward money dropped to $1 per homer. Kittle kept slugging.

"Then it went down to a quarter," he said. "I was hitting too many."

Some kids got paid for cutting the lawn. This was Kittle's way to earn an allowance. Kittle also noticed a pattern that continued through his Major-League career. He hit more of his home runs, and the biggest blasts, off the best pitchers. The same principle applied in professional ball, but it did not stand to reason that he would hit more home runs off pitchers who gave up fewer.

"It seemed like every time, even through my big-league career, when I faced mediocre pitchers, I did horrible against them," Kittle said. "It might have just been my attention span. Maybe I was a little goofy."

Kittle enrolled at a nearby private Catholic high school named Andrean with a good sports program.

"They told me that freshmen weren't good enough to make the baseball team and I literally came home crying," Kittle said. "I told my dad. He had just come home from work in the steel mill full of dust and soot. He drove me back to the school and met with an official and said, 'I'll buy uniforms for the whole team if you just let the boy try out.' And they didn't. I wound up transferring (to William Wirt High School) and later I played against that school and in a doubleheader I think I got 14 RBIs."

Kittle said his father was his biggest fan, but also his harshest critic. Playing summer ball when he was about 16, Kittle was at shortstop. He hit five home runs in a doubleheader, but near game's end he performed a flashy maneuver in the field to tease a friend from the other team who hit the ball.

"I was kind of double pumping," Kittle said. "I threw it to first and the first baseman should have caught it, but he missed and the ball hit the fence. The runner stayed at first anyway and we won. But my dad didn't let me eat dinner that night. He said, 'There's good ball and bad ball, but stupid ball is what you did tonight, showing off.'"

Baseball was Kittle's life, but he wanted to make his life center around baseball. After high school, he attended a try-out camp in Laporte, Indiana. It was a mass casting call, with some 200 hopefuls on the field.

"You have to have a good day to get looked at," Kittle said. "I hit home run after home run. They go, 'What position do you play?' I go, 'Where do you want me to play?'"

The Los Angeles Dodgers liked Kittle best. Playing in the minors in 1977, Kittle complained of headaches and back pain. It turned out he broke his neck. He suffered two crushed vertebrae that caused a pinched nerve in his neck and paralysis in his right arm. Kittle's season ended and he was sure his career had, too, after spinal fusion surgery sidelined him for four months. It took time to recuperate and, because the Dodgers released him, he had no team in 1978. Kittle, still only 19, started as an iron worker and signed up for the company baseball team. He began lighting up the sandlots with home runs.

Word trickled down the turnpike from northern Indiana to the south side of Chicago, and a special tryout was arranged at Comiskey Park in the fall of 1978 by former Sox star pitcher Billy Pierce, who saw Kittle hit. This time Kittle was not surrounded by 200 wannabes. The Sox wanted to see if he was an exaggerated local legend who was the star of the mills, or if he truly had potential to make the shift into pay-for-play ball. The tryout in front of team owner Bill Veeck was a glorious success—he said, "Don't let him leave the park without signing him." It took Kittle four years to make the majors, but by the time he was placed on the White Sox roster at the end of spring training of 1983, his reputation as a slugger preceded him.

THE SETTING

Kittle was an unheralded signee when he joined the White Sox organization. He was on his second chance and there was little correlation between how he performed in semi-pro ball to going head to head with professional pitching. Still, twice Kittle had been plucked off sandlots by professional scouts who saw beyond his youth and limited experience to a hearty-sized man who could powder the ball to adjoining zip codes.

Kittle cut a Paul Bunyan-like swath through the minors, belting tape-measure home runs as he went. By 1982, team officials in Chicago were nodding sagely and sportswriters wrote about Kittle as an up-and-comer. Playing for the AAA Edmonton Trappers, Kittle destroyed Pacific Coast League pitching.

It was obvious Kittle would be spending summers in Chicago when he slugged 50 home runs with 145 RBIs for the Trappers. That kind of performance won him minor league player of the year awards. He was brought up for a cameo in September of 1982 for a little show-and-tell, and Kittle was with the team to stay when the Sox broke camp for their runaway division title season in 1983.

THE GAME OF MY LIFE
BY RON KITTLE

CHICAGO WHITE SOX VS. TEXAS RANGERS, APRIL 5, 1983

The game that means the most and that I enjoyed so much was my first game with the White Sox to start the season in 1983. We were playing the Texas Rangers in Arlington, Texas.

The first game of the season and the first game of the series, I didn't start, but I pinch-hit. The second game I started. And you know what was my biggest thrill? Just getting my name announced by the public address announcer because I was between Greg Luzinski and Carlton Fisk in the lineup. Just hearing my name. It was like confirmation I had made it to the big leagues. Luzinski was batting fourth, I was batting fifth, and Fisk was batting sixth. It was so exciting

158

because it was a reminder of where I was. It was, "Yeah, those are the guys that I was watching on TV for years."

And all of a sudden, my name is being announced with that group. Then the national anthem was played and jets flew over. It was just one of those great days that you can't ever forget. It didn't matter what I did during the game (he was 0-for-3), it was all about being there.

GAME RESULTS

The White Sox lost 4-1 to the Rangers that day. But the fact that it was a fresh, new season at its beginning, struck Kittle and stayed with him. During his 20-game close-out-the-season call-up the previous fall, Kittle hit his first Major-League home run. On the next-to-last day of the season in Minnesota on October 2, Kittle ripped a three-run homer off Twins pitcher Frank Viola. The White Sox won 5-3 that day.

Shortly after the Rangers series, the White Sox returned to Comiskey for the home opener against the Orioles, his dad's old team. There was a loud contingent of pro-Kittle rooters in the stands, including his parents and five siblings and a bunch of people from the neighborhood. After all, he grew up only about 25 miles from the park.

"It was nice having family there," Kittle said. "My friends from high school were there. The park couldn't get any closer to home."

Although the Sox lost the game 10-8, Kittle put on a good show for the old gang, collecting two hits, two runs, and two runs batted in. In fact, Kittle put on a good show for the entire league. On his way to a 35-home run and 100-RBI season, he was the only White Sox player selected for the 1983 All-Star game in Chicago. When Kittle was introduced to the home fans, the applause and standing ovation went on for so long that he had to tip his cap in acknowledgment of the cheers three times.

"I had 25 home runs at the All-Star break," Kittle said. "The team was a little sluggish in the first half, but we had a lot of talent.

Then everyone started picking up the slack and we started winning a lot of ballgames."

In the middle of the season, Kittle was part of a fluke play against the Yankees. Fireballing Goose Gossage came into the game in relief. Kittle came to the plate with the bases loaded.

"He was throwing smoke," Kittle said. "I hit a 3-2 fastball as hard as I've ever hit a ball in my entire life. It was a one-hopper to third that hit Graig Nettles in the chest. It knocked him down and the ball bounced forward. Blood was coming off Graig Nettles' chest because the ball bounced off his crucifix and cut into his chest area.

"I'm standing on first base and Gossage looks over at Nettles and says, 'You couldn't catch shit over there.' Nettles goes, 'You couldn't strike out anybody. Throw. Get the guy out. You're trying to get us killed.' They're out there arguing and I'm having fun and shaking, being excited, nervous. It was so funny. The ball came in at 100 mph and it went out at 100 mph. There was no play on the ball."

REFLECTIONS ON BASEBALL

When Kittle was the focus of so much Chicago attention as a rookie and at the All-Star game, he was asked how he was handling it all.

"I got a bigger hat," he joked.

Kittle loved his year in the limelight. Once that summer, he stopped in to a bank on an errand and ended up sticking around for half an hour signing autographs. Kittle's spectacular ride in 1983 advertised a bright future. Although he had other productive years, Kittle's numbers never reached the stratosphere again. A big reason was injuries. A big man with a big sense of humor and an embracing charm, Kittle was never terribly lucky when it came to hurts interrupting playing time. Kittle felt haunted by the vertebrae problem his whole career and he was still only 33 years old when he retired in 1991 after a final, 17-game fling with the White Sox.

"I probably played my career at about 70 percent of my ability," he said. "I was limited. I went out there and took my pain pills and tried to play and I still had fun. Then other injuries kind of took hold. I have the three vertebrae fused in my neck and I have two others ruptured. I had two completely taken out of my lower back. It just got to the point where I had to work out eight hours a day just to play and I couldn't do it. It just hurt so bad. Retiring was probably the smartest decision I made. Thank God I'm not in a wheelchair."

Kittle said when he hears about what steroids can do for a body, he wonders if he would have been tempted to take them to help prevent from breaking down.

"You know, make myself stronger so I could play longer," he said. "But I was so scared of my dad. As old as he was, he still probably could have kicked my butt. His hands were big paws. He taught me the right thing to do."

Kittle remains affiliated with the White Sox, working in the community relations department. He represents the team at public functions and during the season attends about three games a week during home stands.

"My joke is that my favorite team is always the one that has their logo on my paycheck," he said. "But I like the White Sox. There are a lot of great guys in the organization, from top to bottom. I'm a fan. I follow them. There's nothing better than seeing that scoreboard go off with the fireworks when they hit a home run."

CHAPTER 22

HAROLD BAINES

When Harold Baines was a little kid, baseball was the game to play in the neighborhood. He was about seven when he played on his first Little League team, but he and other kids played pickup games all of the time.

"I think back in the late 1960s and early '70s, your parents told you to stay outside till dark," Baines said. "You really didn't worry about working or anything like that because you really didn't need that much. So we just played. Whatever season it was, we played that sport."

Baines' father, Linwood, a masonry worker who raised his children alone after he split up with Baines' mother, also imparted a great deal of advice—life advice as much as sports advice. During his career, Baines maintained a placid demeanor on the field. He rarely showed emotions that indicated highs or lows. He did his job and didn't showboat.

"The way he raised us," Baines said of his father, "was just to get the job done. We were supposed to be businesslike, and that was on the field, too."

Baines lived in the small Maryland town of St. Michaels, near Easton, which happened to be where White Sox owner Bill Veeck took his family to live the first time he surrendered operations of the team for health reasons, and he maintained a home there.

"Bill Veeck discovered me," Baines said. "I just think I was in the right spot at the right time."

Baines said he was later told Veeck first saw him play in a Little League game when he was 12 and was intrigued by his skill, and that Veeck followed his career from a distance until Baines was 18. Then the White Sox made Baines their No. 1 draft pick. The White Sox signed Baines and after fortuitously playing under Tony La Russa in AA, he made it to the majors in 1980. The player and manager were on the upward climb through the minors together.

"He had the job and he knew my ability," Baines said. "The White Sox didn't have a set outfield, so I was able to come to spring training and win a job."

A job, it turned out, that would last for 22 years.

THE SETTING

Baines played in 141 games as a rookie in 1980. He was still feeling his way in the majors and while he had some big hits, his was not a dominant bat in the Sox lineup.

In 1983, Baines was a regular on the fondly remembered Sox "Winning Ugly" team with its 99 wins and playoff experience. By 1984, Baines was established and poised to break out with a string of All-Star-caliber seasons.

There are 162 regularly scheduled games in each team's season and one of the things baseball fans appreciate about the sport is how different the games are. No matter how long a spectactor has been a fan of the game there is always a chance when he goes to a ballpark that he will see something he has never seen happen on the diamond. It might be something monumental like a perfect game. It might he something fantastic for an individual player. Or it might be something that ends up etched in the team record book. Any game that takes two days to complete is competing for space in the record book. And the White Sox's 25-inning game against the Milwaukee Brewers is the longest in team history. There is no telling how long the game might have lasted if Baines hadn't ended it when he did.

THE GAME OF MY LIFE
BY HAROLD BAINES

CHICAGO WHITE SOX VS. MILWAUKEE BREWERS, MAY 8-9, 1984.

It was over a two-day period. That was pretty unusual. As a player I've been involved in nothing else close to that. It did feel a little like two separate games really because we went home and then came back and played another nine innings. It was part of yesterday's game, but we only had to play part of a game. We had another game to play that day. We walked off the field at Comiskey Park and went home to sleep. When we came back, we just wanted it to end as quickly as it could because we had another game. But we battled to the end. It was in the beginning of the season, so it was just another game. It's just a game, period.

The game started at a regular night starting time and it didn't end until the next night. I came to the plate in the bottom of the 25th inning and I hit one really good. The home run ended the game. The Brewers went up a couple of runs in the top of the 21st inning, but we were able to score again and tie it. We had brought Tom Seaver into the game in relief in the top of the 25th—a 300-game winner—and he got the win.

I'm the type of guy who never really shows a lot of emotion, so I didn't run around the bases fist-pumping or stuff like that. I was thankful to have the opportunity to hit the home run, but I keep most of my emotions inside.

GAME RESULTS

Baines won the game 7-6 for the White Sox with a 420-foot shot off losing pitcher Chuck Porter. It was the 753rd pitch of an eight-hour, six-minute game, the longest in Major League history. Fourteen hurlers shared in the pitch count.

The game started on a Tuesday when 17 innings were played and ended on a Wednesday when it took eight more to be decided. It was just past 1 a.m. with the score 3-3, when the game was suspended for the rest of the night. When the contest ended, Baines' bat was shipped to the National Baseball Hall of Fame in Cooperstown, New York. If Baines was not overly excited, La Russa seemed to be. He's the one who scooped up the bat, recognizing the potential historical significance. In terms of innings, it is the second longest game ever played. The Boston Braves and the Brooklyn Dodgers played to a 26-inning, 1-1 tie in 1920.

Right after the suspended game was completed, the regularly scheduled game for May 9 began. Seaver was the starter, went 8⅓ innings, and ended up with two victories on his resume in the same day. The White Sox recorded 23 hits and the Brewers 20 in the 25-inning adventure. Some players—Fisk and Vance Law for the White Sox, and Cecil Cooper for Milwaukee—had 11 official at-bats in the game. Normally that is the accumulation of three games work. Paid attendance was 14,754, though it is impossible to count how many fans sat through all 25 innings.

REFLECTING ON BASEBALL

Few people can make the claim that they were on hand for a 25-inning game at any level of play, and if a fan sees one he's not going to forget it.

"People in Chicago and Milwaukee remember that game," Baines said, "because I get people all of the time who say they were at that game. They don't say if they were there for the whole thing. They never really go into that. They just say they remember me and the home run in the 25th inning."

Baines came to work every day for 22 years dreaming of being part of a team that advanced to the World Series and would provide him with a championship ring. It never happened. But he had many other playing highlights.

In 1982, when he was only 23, Baines hit three home runs in a single game against the Detroit Tigers. The fans went crazy, but once again Baines showed little exuberance. On a day he compiled six RBIs, his teammates had to shove him out of the dugout to acknowledge the cheering crowd. He was just being businesslike.

Baines matched the feat with a three-homer game against Minnesota, on the road, in 1984. Quiet and unassuming, it is no surprise that Baines maintains his off-season home in St. Michaels, where he is raising his four children. Every January 9 in St. Michaels, there is a Harold Baines Day. But it is more of a carnival day with charitable events than a day to honor the favorite son.

The softspoken Baines carried a big stick, retiring with 384 home runs 1,628 RBIs, and a .289 average. He was a six-time All-Star. Baines would have preferred to play his entire career with the White Sox, and he always carried the Sox in his heart, so it seemed logical he would return to his favorite organization after retiring in 2001. Baines became a minor-league field instructor for the franchise and worked on scouting and player development before becoming a full-time coach in 2004. He completed his fourth season on the staff of manager Ozzie Guillen, his one-time teammate, in 2007. Baines loves coaching and sees it as his proper post-playing role above managing.

"I think you have to be very outspoken to be a manager," Baines said. "I'm very introverted, so I don't think I would be right for it. I mean I can argue if I have to, but that's not my nature. I just like to stay in my comfort zone and I know my comfort zone isn't as a manager."

White Sox coaching was definitely more in Baines' comfort zone.

"When I finished playing, I knew that my love was still baseball and I knew I wanted to give something back to the game because it gave me so much as a player, especially this organization," he said. "It gave me the opportunity to play baseball. I wanted to give back the knowledge I learned to the present players. They like me and gave me a job to coach. I consider this to be my home."

Baines' second chance at a World Series came as a coach in 2005. The White Sox won the title and Baines got a ring, reminding him that anything can happen in baseball, even 25-inning games. And that one day, perhaps, there will be a 27-inning game breaking all records.

"With human beings you never know what will happen," Baines said. "We're not machines, so on that given day you never know who's going to be good and who's going to be bad. When you're dealing with human beings you never know what will happen."

CHAPTER 23

LaMARR HOYT

Growing up in Columbia, South Carolina, where he still lives, Dewey LaMarr Hoyt was a superb all-around athlete, but he also got into trouble often. After his parents split up, Hoyt was raised by an aunt. He was frequently in fights, running with a street gang, and had a reputation as someone who would finish fights quickly with punches to the face. Sports steered him in a more productive direction. At Keenan High School, Hoyt played football, basketball, and baseball, and he made fans gasp with his long-distance punts, often kicking the ball 50 yards. He hesitates to say he was a better baseball player than punter.

"I'd say that one came just as easily as the other," he said. "I was just as good in basketball, baseball, and football. My senior year I started at quarterback, was a linebacker, I kicked off, and I punted. I quit playing basketball my junior year."

Hoyt was not thinking about professional baseball after high school. He was thinking about playing one or more of his favorite sports at Duke or Clemson.

"The only school in the southeast that didn't recruit me was South Carolina, which I thought was kind of weird," Hoyt said.

However, the New York Yankees drafted Hoyt in the fifth round, gave him $25,000 and offered him the chance to play right away in rookie ball in Johnson City, Tennessee. At first, Hoyt thought it would be a good experience. But he panicked when he got to Tennessee.

"I checked into the hotel and I remember the rooms were just gigantic and the ceilings were about 30 feet high," Hoyt said. "I sat down on the bed and I'm thinking, 'Shouldn't somebody call me or something?' Nothing happened and I got disenchanted."

Hoyt sat around the hotel for three hours, checked out and drove four hours home to South Carolina.

"They called about three days later looking for me," Hoyt said, "and they said, 'We hope he's there because he's not here.' My mother said, 'He's here. Do you want to talk to him?' So they talked me into coming back."

Eventually, Hoyt ended up White Sox property in a trade that sent shortstop Bucky Dent to the Yankees. Hoyt needed time in the minors to mature and learn. He was confident but savvy, with a good memory, and when he faced hitters in the minors he remembered strengths and weaknesses. Hoyt also played winter ball for Tony La Russa and got their relationship off to a good start.

In an era before opposing batters' tendencies were so thoroughly studied, recorded on film and pitching charts, Hoyt kept many of his opinions and records in his head. Hoyt had faced Eddie Murray in the early 1970s when they were both fledgling ballplayers. And then he faced him again in a crucial circumstance during the 1983 play-offs.

"I was with the Yankees out of Johnson City and he was with Bluefield, West Virginia, the Orioles' rookie league team," Hoyt recalled. "He couldn't hit the broad side of a barn if you threw him a breaking ball. Next time I saw him he's in the Major Leagues, he's a switch hitter and I wondered what he had learned to hit. I just banged him inside with fastballs."

At a critical juncture in a playoff game, La Russa wanted to remove Hoyt from the game. Hoyt remembered Murray's tendencies. He knew when Murray warmed up with his swings he'd hunch into a certain stance if he was looking for a change-up. In a one-minute exchange on the mound he convinced La Russa he had all of this secret knowledge about a future Hall of Fame hitter that could save the game.

"He tips off what he's looking for," Hoyt said to La Russa. "If you don't mind would you turn around and go back to the dugout and just let me get him out?"

La Russa told him to forget it, he was bringing in a reliever. Hoyt was sure he could get Murray out. La Russa warned Hoyt, "You know, we've got a lot riding on this." Murray assumed his stance and Hoyt ran a fastball inside. Murray swung, made minimal contact, and broke his bat. But his weak roller was so slow he almost got an infield hit.

"If it hadn't been for Julio Cruz being as quick as he was. . ." Hoyt said. "He came in and scooped the ball up with one hand and threw Eddie out by a step and that game was over."

After the game, La Russa talked hitters with Hoyt and Hoyt said he knew some quirk or habit about nearly half the hitters in the American League.

"My whole philosophy is that when they step in the box, if they're going to give me a certain part of the strike zone, I'm gonna take it, and until they adjust, I'm going to keep pounding away," Hoyt said. "I'm throwing everything but what they want to see. A good memory comes in handy lots of times."

THE SETTING

Hoyt had ups and downs in the minors, and it wasn't just switching from Class AAA to Class A. He came within a whisker of giving up pro baseball in his first hours in Johnson City. He was ready to retire a couple of years later when the White Sox wanted to send him to Class A Appleton, Wisconsin even though he had won 20 games at that level the season before. He thought his baseball career was on a dead-end street. Once again Hoyt thought about trying college football. He also had a friend in the home-building business who might give him a job.

Hoyt became a consistent winner in the minors and had a productive winter in the Dominican Republic in 1978 under La Russa, then made his Majoreague debut in 1979 with the Sox. By 1980, Hoyt was a regular starter and finished 9-3. He showed more and more poise and in 1982 emerged from a pack of young pitchers as staff workhorse, going 19-15. When the 1983 season began, Hoyt was the staff ace. He was a burly man and, in a true rarity, wore a thick beard. In an early-season game against the Yankees, before the White Sox got hot and moved away from the field in the American League West, Hoyt pitched the game of his life.

THE GAME OF MY LIFE
BY LAMARR HOYT

CHICAGO WHITE SOX VS. NEW YORK YANKEES, MAY 2, 1984

It was in early May against the Yankees at Comiskey Park and it was probably the best game I ever pitched in the Major Leagues. I only faced 27 hitters in the entire game (the minimum for a nine-inning, complete game). I got through seven innings without giving up a hit and in the top of the eighth inning Don Mattingly came to bat.

There are a few games when you walk out there and you know you've got your best stuff. And I knew it from the opening pitch of the game that day. I didn't look up until about the seventh inning and realized what was going on. All the guys were starting to stay away from me.

The objective in every start, I felt, was to pitch a perfect game and see how far into the game I could get before they got to me. That was the recurring theme of every start. Sometimes they got you early, sometimes they got you in the middle, but you tried to minimize whatever they did against you. I'm throwing these real hard sinkers and breaking balls and they're just not on me at all. I knew I had them and then it was just a matter of whether I could get to the end of the game.

Mattingly hit a little dying quail off the end of his bat to left field. Ron Kittle was our left fielder. He was a better hitter than fielder. I don't want to say anything too bad about it because it was a ball that he could have caught. Kittle broke back because he saw that Mattingly swung really hard. Being on the mound you know he didn't make good contact. It was just a squibber off the end of the bat. Kittle broke back to the wall and our shortstop, Jerry Dybzinksi, ran out to short left field. The ball ended up falling right between them.

The next guy up was Steve Kemp and on the first pitch I threw him he hit a one-hopper back to me. I promptly turned a double play. So with the next guy out I only faced 27 hitters. The only base runner was Mattingly on that little ding of a hit. I consider it a perfect game. Unfortunately, Don Mattingly dumped a little single over there in left.

GAME RESULTS

The game went into the books as a one-hitter for Hoyt, who also struck out eight men. The White Sox won 3-0, defeating Jose Rijo. Hoyt said he always knew when he gave up a hit or walk to allow the first base runner in a game. It was part of his general awareness and goal to outsmart batters since he didn't have the liveliest fastball in the sport.

"I remembered because fortunately the thing that aided me more than anything else was my capability or facility for memory," Hoyt said.

Going into the 1983 season, the White Sox knew that Hoyt was going to be one of their key pitchers, but they didn't know he would be much better than that. That summer Hoyt was the best pitcher in the American League, finishing with a 24-10 record and capturing the Cy Young Award.

"To be honest, we were getting off to a start that was the opposite of the year before," Hoyt said. "I was kind of mad because my statistics as far as hits and innings ratio and strikeouts and innings-pitched ratio and walks were good, but we just weren't scoring runs.

It's frustrating for a pitcher. I was a little bit pissed off before the game even started."

Despite being an excellent all-around player and a batting title champ, Mattingly was not a particular nemesis for Hoyt. However, Hoyt always got psyched up to pitch against the Yankees.

"Because it was the organization I came from, I just kind of felt like I needed to show them that I was not in the right uniform," Hoyt said. "I kind of pitched against them that way."

It was a season when little went wrong. Hoyt won his final 13 decisions as the Sox steamrolled to their 20-game lead in the standings. In 260⅔ innings pitched he walked just 31 hitters, four intentionally—a phenomenal exhibition of control.

In spring training of 1984, Hoyt signed a six-year contract that called for $1 million a year, which at the time was the richest ever for a pitcher.

REFLECTIONS ON BASEBALL

Hoyt was in his prime when he won 24 games for the White Sox and he and the team looked forward to many more fruitful years in partnership. But it did not work out that way. The next season, Hoyt's record was 13-18. A controversial trade (the key incoming player was Ozzie Guillen) shipped Hoyt to San Diego, where he had a nice 16-8 season in 1985 and then was out of the majors for good after 1986. Tearing three tendons ruined Hoyt's throwing shoulder. Trouble with drug use contributed to waylaying Hoyt's career when he was arrested three times and served jail time.

Eventually Hoyt cleaned up his life, married, had three children, and stayed out of baseball until 2001, when he worked at a White Sox fantasy camp in Arizona. In 2004, Hoyt was invited to help out at White Sox spring training and he developed a strong appreciation for Mark Buehrle's pitching.

"He's a bulldog out there," Hoyt said. "I like his whole approach. He pitches like I would like to, or like I used to. He sets the pace of the game. I just love his attitude."

The White Sox of 1983 were a dominant team in the regular season, but lost their playoff round to the Baltimore Orioles three games to one. It was as close as a White Sox team got to the World Series for many surrounding decades.

"I felt if we could have just gotten one more win and I could have gotten another start, we could have been in the World Series," Hoyt said. "Both teams knew that whichever team won was going to beat the Phillies in the World Series. But you know, it's just one of those things. We just didn't hit for three games and that eliminated us for the season. We were totally, 100 percent, into grinding it out the whole way."

Hoyt was happy for the organization when the White Sox of 2005 did go all the way.

"I was so glad they won the World Series," he said.

Hoyt sells golf clubs for the Dick's Sporting Goods chain and makes some sports memorabilia show appearances signing autographs. Hoyt has a couple of baseball-playing boys—Matthew, 13, and Joshua, 10. He doesn't push them, but encourages them.

"Both of them show they have the ability (to be good)," Hoyt said. Every once in a while, Matthew, who is an ESPN nut, sees a classic game they have on and watches me pitch against somebody. And he's seen some of the tapes around the house. I haven't shown him this or shown him that, but the little one has a good pitching arm. He's got a world of talent. I can tell already. He's got the instincts. You can tell when a kid has the instincts. They say that it's in the genes and that's why a lot of ex-Major League players have their kids get drafted."

Hoyt visits Chicago a few times a year, and until the White Sox won the Series in 2005 he regularly ran into fans who reminisced about 1983 and how they wish he had got the ball one more time.

"They say, 'My God, what would have happened if you could have gotten another start?' And we could have gone down the road."

Pitching the Sox into the World Series certainly would have been the ultimate capper to the best baseball season of LaMarr Hoyt's career.

CHAPTER 24

TADAHITO IGUCHI

Tadahito Iguchi was born and raised in Tokyo where he aspired to play professional baseball in the Japan League. A graduate of Kokugakuin Kugayama High School, Iguchi was a highly respected player at a young age. Iguchi's older brother Nobukabu was a baseball player and Tadahito tagged along to watch him play. When he was old enough, Iguchi started playing in the equivalent of the American Little League and was tutored and influenced by his coach, Mitsuo Ikochi.

"I just naturally started to play the game and then I got to love the game," Iguchi said through his interpreter, David Yamamoto.

After high school, Iguchi attended Aoyama Gakuin University and set a Tokyo Metropolitan University record by hitting 24 home runs. He was also a Triple Crown winner, leading his league in average, home runs, and RBIs, and was selected Most Valuable Player.

Baseball has a long history in Japan. Tours by American Major Leaguers were conducted well before World War II and the post-war American presence helped promote the game. Later, American players near the end of their careers began playing a few seasons in Japan. Some Americans even became stars. About a decade ago, Japanese players began attempting the crossover in the other direction. An early success story was pitcher Hideo Nomo with the Los Angeles Dodgers, the author of a Major League no-hitter.

The player who symbolized the closing of the gap in talent and showed that transferring Japanese players could do well was Ichiro Suzuki, the instant star with the Seattle Mariners, who has won American League batting titles and set the all-time Major League single-season hits record. He truly paved the way for Japanese players to believe that they could make it in the U.S.

In 1997, Iguchi broke into the Japan Major Leagues with the Fukuoka Daiei Hawks and although he did not have a sterling season at the plate, batting .203 in 76 games, he made only four errors. Iguchi became a more accomplished hitter as he went along. He had a 30-home-run season. He had a 100 RBI season. His average increased. As he improved, Iguchi began thinking he might like to give playing in the majors a shot.

THE SETTING

In the off-season leading up to the 2005 campaign, White Sox general manager Kenny Williams believed his team needed to beef up at second base. He had a strong pitching rotation, good power in the lineup, and a belief that he had put together a roster that could contend for the postseason. But he was worried about second base. Williams examined his farm system and did not see a prospect. He explored trades with other Major League teams. He checked on available free agents.

And then he did what nobody expected. He signed a free agent from Japan named Tadahito Iguchi who was unknown in Chicago and among baseball fans around the United States. Williams had done his due diligence and he saw in the 30-year-old rookie a guy who could step in right away and play every day.

For $3.2 million, Williams signed Iguchi and it didn't take long for manager Ozzie Guillen to plug him into the starting lineup. Iguchi didn't speak much English and needed an interpreter in the clubhouse, but he spoke universally with his bat and glove. Iguchi had eyed other Japanese stars making good in the United States and thought he might be able to break in as well and make more money for his family than he could in Japan. He played his cards right, becoming available after hitting .333 in 124 games during the 2004 season.

"Of course I used to dream of coming to play in the Major Leagues," Iguchi said in the White Sox clubhouse during the summer of 2007. "But I had no clue as to where I was going to end up. I had some knowledge of the White Sox, but I had no idea I was going to end up with the White Sox."

In spring training, Iguchi made a solid impression on Guillen, a man who had been a middle infielder himself, and when the Sox opened the season in early April against the Cleveland Indians, Iguchi was a starter. The moment he had waited for so long was at hand.

THE GAME OF MY LIFE
BY TADAHITO IGUCHI

CHICAGO WHITE SOX VS. CLEVELAND INDIANS, APRIL 4, 2005

I always had dreamed of coming here and playing (in the United States) and the day had finally come. There was somewhat of an opening ceremony since it was the opening of the season. The fans were all different than they were in Japan, very loud, and the excitement kept building up, up, up.

As I waited for the game to start I had the feeling going through me that I was finally here to fulfill my dreams. But what I really remember about this game was my first at-bat. I actually struck out and was hitless in the game. I struck out swinging at a pitch. I had a feeling in my heart that I was unsatisfied with what I did that day. But I think that I used that as motivation for later on.

Although I wasn't satisfied with what I did that day it was a relief that I got my first day as a Major Leaguer in and that I had my first game. It's a long season. There are 162 games. I felt that the hits would come later on. It was more of a feeling of relief for me when the game was over.

GAME RESULTS

The White Sox defeated the Cleveland Indians, 1-0, in the season opener. Iguchi went 0-for-4 at the plate. Besides the strikeout, Iguchi went down on a foul popup and two grounders hit to third.

By officially competing in the game, Iguchi became the 24th Japanese player to play in the majors. He was not a barrier breaker, but his arrival was still news in Japan. Like so many other contemporary Japanese ballplayers, Iguchi earned his own full-time contingent of Japanese print and video reporters following him around. They reported on everything he did, from tying his shoelaces to where he ate and, naturally, how he played.

Iguchi's second game two days later gave the home folks more to cheer about. The White Sox beat the Indians again, 4-3, and besides a walk in his first at-bat, Iguchi collected his first Major League hit. He stroked a double to left field in the sixth inning.

The news kept getting better. Iguchi was more of a primary hitter in the lineup in Japan, but Guillen placed him second in the White Sox batting order and he became a table setter for the sluggers. Iguchi was asked to bunt more, move runners over with the hit-and-run, and sacrifice much of his game. Still, Iguchi batted .278 with 15 home runs and 71 RBIs. By anyone's measure, his transition from baseball in Japan to baseball in the United States was a success.

Iguchi became popular with White Sox fans who chanted, "Gooch, Gooch," when he stepped into the batter's box and he was pleased with himself when he cracked a game-winning three-run homer against the Boston Red Sox.

"That game was where I was most satisfied," Iguchi said.

Never in those dreams Iguchi nurtured over the years in Japan did he envision winning the World Series in his first season in the United States. That came later—his rookie season when the Sox swept the Houston Astros to win the title.

"I was most excited about that when it was done and we clinched the world championship," Iguchi said. "That was the best game. First, when we won, when we became champions, to me it was an unbelievable feeling that something like that was happening in my first year. The feeling of becoming a champion didn't sink in until after the parade."

The White Sox captured their first World Series crown in 88 years, and Chicago celebrated with great energy. The parade that wound through the city streets honoring the White Sox attracted an estimated two million fans. Thankful for the unselfish way Iguchi contributed, Guillen said the new player was the team MVP.

"When he came to the United States he had to change his game for us, and he did," Guillen said. "This kid does everything for the team and that's why I keep saying this kid is my MVP."

REFLECTIONS ON BASEBALL

In many ways, Iguchi turned in an even better season in 2006 when the Sox won 90 games but missed the playoffs. His batting average was up three points, to .281. He hit three more home runs, or 18, and drove in 67 runs, four less while committing only eight errors, six fewer than in the pennant-winning year.

Iguchi, his wife, Asumi, and five-year-old daughter, Rio, moved to Schaumburg, a suburb about 25 miles west of Chicago. The community has a thriving Japanese community. He became a regular visitor to the Japanese market in Arlington Heights and was even more popular among Japanese-American baseball fans than the general White Sox fan.

Although English is not Iguchi's first language and he relied on interpreters for much of his daily life outside the ballpark (as well as handling interviews at U.S. Cellular Field), Iguchi does understand quite a bit of English. The story goes that in spring training, when he first met Guillen who is from Venezuela and speaks English with a Latino accent, the manager asked if he spoke English. Iguchi said, "No." Guillen laughed and said, "Me neither."

When the 2007 season began, Iguchi, in the final year of his three-year deal with the White Sox, was once again the regular second baseman. But he got off to a bad start, hitting only .220 over the first two months of the season. He said he was playing in pain with an injured left index finger, but felt he should play through it and not rest.

Soon it became obvious that while Iguchi's lack of production was slowing down the White Sox offense, he was far from the only problem. Several players started slowly. It was almost a group slump. Pitchers were off. Players got hurt. The Sox were up-and-down, seemingly playing far under their potential. The outstanding rotation that had carried Chicago to the 2005 World Series championship performed poorly, and fans and team officials became frustrated.

Amazingly, the team that figured to contend for the American League Central Division title tumbled into last place. In mid-season, with star second baseman Chase Utley injured, the Philadelphia Phillies traded an unknown minor league pitcher to the White Sox for Iguchi and plugged him into their lineup. The trade occurred on July 27 and Iguchi was in the locker room, dressing for a game when he was informed. Stunned and shocked, Iguchi had tears in his eyes when he said goodbye to Guillen in his office.

"I really wanted to stay here in Chicago," Iguchi told reporters. "I had no idea something like this was going to happen."

Iguchi gave the Phillies a lift over the season's last two months and they qualified for the playoffs. But Iguchi's contract was up, making him a free agent. He said he hoped the White Sox might sign him again, but that didn't happen and he joined the San Diego Padres.

Besides being comfortable in the Chicago area, the White Sox had provided Iguchi with a very special baseball memory. After participating in the World Series parade, Iguchi had a better sense of how important the triumph was to the community and how swiftly he had risen to the top in just a single season with the team.

"It was kind of unbelievable," Iguchi said. "After the parade I looked back thinking, 'Wow!'"

CHAPTER 25

JIM THOME

Jim Thome grew up in Central Illinois and early on became a passionate, involved outdoorsman who loves to hunt and fish. He started playing baseball in Little League at seven or eight. He was smitten with the game and played catch often with his father, Chuck.

"My dad and I practiced a lot and I was successful playing just about right away," Thome said. "I wanted to play baseball from day one after I started doing it. I was just a huge, huge baseball fan. We followed the Cubs since I was from Illinois and they were on TV all of the time on WGN."

WGN brought the Cubs into many living rooms in many states, making Cubs fans out of long-distance baseball followers like the Thome family. Between work and school schedules, Thome, his dad, and his grandfather rooted for the team. Thome's father, a foreman, spent 39 years working for Caterpillar.

"We would sit there together and watch Cubs games, and it was pretty cool," Thome said.

At the time, Thome enjoyed watching Bill Buckner and especially Dave Kingman when he hit his towering home runs that seemed to land in the next county. Ironically, even though he became one of the greatest home-run hitters in the history of the sport, Thome was not a serious home-run hitter growing up.

"Actually, it wasn't until I was in AAA when I started hitting homers," Thome said.

The men in the family, including Thome's brother, all enjoyed the outdoors. The older generations introduced Jim and Chuck to bluegill and bass fishing, and then other sporting pursuits.

"It was good growing up in the Midwest," Thome said. "You were definitely presented to the outdoors, no question."

Thome graduated from Limestone High School where he was All-State in basketball and baseball and attended Illinois Central College, where he also played both sports. Years later, the school named its baseball stadium after Thome.

Coming from a close family is something Thome always considered a blessing, but it was possible his mother, Joyce, who died of lung cancer in 2005, was a bigger fan of his than any other relative. She attended 11 straight Major League opening day games her son played in and sent Jim home-baked cookies when he was in a slump. Joyce saved her son's baseball newspaper clippings and memorabilia.

As a little guy, Thome might have cheered the hardest for the Cubs, but as he moved into his mid-30s with a distinguished career under his belt with the Indians and Phillies, Thome was thrilled to move close to home when he was traded to the White Sox in 2005 as their new designated hitter.

It felt right to everybody. White Sox fans welcomed an Illinois player with the reputation not only as a premier slugger, but as one of the nicest people in baseball. His father and relatives in Peoria relished the idea that Thome's home games would be close to his home, where he still lives in the off-season. And his wife Andrea and daughter also appreciated that going to Chicago felt like an extension of being in Peoria year-round.

Thome's wife said she thought Thome's mom, who died earlier in the year, was watching over them and helped make the trade possible. When he met the media, Thome repeatedly commented that he thought the whole idea of coming "home" and playing in Chicago was pretty neat.

THE SETTING

It is generally believed that joining the White Sox for the 2006 season represented the last act of Jim Thome's Major League career. He had established himself as a star with the Cleveland Indians and endeared himself to the Philadelphia Phillies. After the White Sox won the World Series with long-time star Frank Thomas on the injured list, they went shopping for a new designated hitter.

There was some risk involved because Thome suffered injuries, too. He was no longer going to be an all-around player. Turning 36 during the season, the 6-foot-4, 225-pound Thome was slated to become a full-time designated hitter. And that is the role he played in 2006, making himself a fan favorite immediately, with his crunch-time hits and massive long-distance blows. Thome finished his first White Sox season with 42 home runs and 109 RBIs. Injuries limited Thome to only 59 games with the Phillies the season before, but his success with Chicago earned him the comeback player of the year award.

Nobody minded that Thome, who had to nurse sensitive hamstrings, didn't play the field. However, there was a pervasive worry that he might get hurt again, which did occur at the beginning of the 2007 season. Nearly eight weeks into the 2007 season, Thome had only played in 22 games. He suffered a strain on the right side of his rib cage swinging a bat too hard.

It was the kind of frustrating minor injury often attributed to an older player as a sign—true or not—that the body is aging and on the verge of a breakdown. Such talk never sits well with a player, especially a star, and when Thome was cleared to rejoin the White Sox lineup, he wanted to show people right away that he was back to his old self.

Most of Thome's career highlights played out in the spotlight in Cleveland, with some special moments added in Philadelphia. His White Sox career was so short it was much harder to find special games to reminisce about, but even though it was neither a World Series nor playoff moment, Thome's return to the Sox lineup as a healthy everyday player was notable to him. He had been out of action 15 days on the disabled list, wondered about the sharpness of his conditioning and had not hit a home run in nearly five weeks. He had played in just one game since returning and thoroughly enjoyed his breakout statement.

THE GAME OF MY LIFE
BY JIM THOME

CHICAGO WHITE SOX VS. OAKLAND A'S, MAY 23, 2007

When you come off the disabled list like that you want to be healthy, first of all, and ready to go. You want to try to contribute in any way you can. You don't know what's going to happen. I didn't know I would go 3-for-3 and hit a home run against Oakland. Fortunately, that was a good night and it kind of exemplifies baseball. There are going to be good nights and decent at-bats and not so good nights.

I think in the long haul, if you just approach it and try to be consistent and not panic during the lows or get too high during the highs when things are going good, you'll be OK. Baseball kind of does that to you. The longer you play it, you realize both sides of it. Even the good times, you enjoy them, but also you've got to forget about them because there's the next day.

This game came at a great time. There is always a little uncertainty about what's going to happen when you come back. You definitely want to get back into a rhythm. You want that rhythm back fast, so the timing of it, getting three hits and driving in five runs, was very good. It's very tough to regain rhythm and timing and keep it. It's one of the toughest things to do in sports. It's a game of change, and one day is so different from the other. When you do hit that little bit of a hot streak you want to really ride it out as long as you can.

It's just nice to contribute. It feels good to be part of that. The great thing about baseball is that we're all a little piece of the puzzle. It's a special thing when you can come back and help.

GAME RESULTS

The White Sox defeated Oakland, 10-4, and Thome's slugging performance with three hits and five RBIs lifted Chicago to a three-game winning streak. At the time, the team was sluggish at bat, so Thome's explosion was very timely. It was a great confidence booster because Thome felt he was not really in game shape. Yet he could still turn in a virtually perfect night at the plate. The showing was significicant for another reason as well—the type of injury Thome incurred could be lingering, easily re-aggravated, and something that might gnaw on a batter mentally to get him to hold back when swinging.

"When you hurt it on a swing," Thome said, "there's going to be doubt until you know you can swing and feel good. One thing about baseball is that one guy doesn't do it all."

Thome demonstrated in that game that he was back at full strength.

"It helps you feel comfortable," he said. "Having a game like that helps you feel comfortable and eases the worry. You can't get too high, as I said, but there is a little bit of peace of mind mentally knowing, 'I did this. I'm feeling good now.' And then you hope you can carry it on to the next day."

Despite being slowed by injury, Thome, who got stronger and better as the season wore on, finished his 2007 White Sox campaign with 35 home runs and 96 RBIs.

REFLECTIONS ON BASEBALL

In the closing month of the 2007 season, Thome reached a long-sought milestone. He has 10 seasons of 40-plus home runs, but on September 16, against the Los Angeles Angels, Thome blasted his 500th homer at U.S. Cellular Field. The number 500 flashed on the video board in the outfield and teammates lifted Thome onto their shoulders on the field. Adding to the emotion of that day, Thome smashed a 3-2 fastball in the ninth inning to win the game, 9-7. Manager Ozzie Guillen said afterwards that he had been sitting next to Sox outfielder Jermaine Dye in the dugout and predicted Thome was going to hit the homer.

"I called it," Guillen said. "I told him, 'Watch this. This kid is going to hit a home run to win the game.' Good things happen to good people and you've got it right there."

Reaching 500 home runs is a special milestone, with only 23 players gathering that many in their careers, and it usually means the player is a shoo-in for the Hall of Fame. During the season, Guillen routinely took to calling Thome a future Hall of Famer, albeit saying Thome would go into the Hall wearing an Indians cap.

"It's amazing, it really is," Thome said after the game and the achivement, "Like a movie script. I would never have imagined doing it in that situation."

One more irony—the free fan treat giveaway for that game was a Jim Thome bobblehead doll. Afterwards, home plate was removed and presented to Thome. The next day—a White Sox off-day—Thome began preparing mementos of the occasion for White Sox employees, autographing photographs of the 500th home run, and more than 150 employees received them. Thome said in the off-season he wanted to take a long, leisurely drive to Cooperstown, New York with his father to present the ball from his 500th home run to the National Baseball Hall of Fame.

The slugger finished the season on an upswing, feeling good and hitting well with 507 homers, and was not mentioning any thoughts about retirement. Thome wanted to help the White Sox win another World Series, but doesn't know how long he will play or if he wants to stay in baseball in another capacity.

"I try to live it day to day and we'll figure out that stuff later on," Thome said.

One thing Jim Thome does know is that after his playing days are over he will have more free time for hunting and fishing.

CHAPTER 26

FRANK THOMAS

Frank Thomas was a big kid who could use his body to his advantage playing sports while growing up in Georgia. He truly excelled at baseball and football. He had power, strength, and good reflexes, and when he grew to his full size, standing 6-foot-5 and weighing around 270 pounds, he could wreak havoc on the gridiron with his body and wreak havoc on the diamond with his bat.

The second youngest of six children growing up in the hot southern city of Columbus, Thomas was closest to his sister Pamela (more than six years younger), and was scarred by her death at two and a half from leukemia. In high school, Thomas trained hard, lifted weights, and ate well to sculpt any hint of flab into muscle. As good as he was in baseball, college football recruiters in the region admired his physique more, and Thomas accepted a scholarship to Auburn when he didn't get drafted by the majors coming out of high school.

At Auburn University in Alabama, Thomas played tight end on a football team with the spectacular running back Bo Jackson, who gained fame with the Oakland Raiders and who played pro football and baseball simultaneously. Thomas improved more in baseball than football, leading the Southeastern Conference in hitting with a .385 average as a sophomore. He won another league batting title at Auburn as a junior and represented the United States in the Pan American Games.

Thomas was determined to make his livelihood and his name in that sport while everyone who didn't know him felt he would play football.

"I was frustrated coming out of high school," Thomas said once. "Longevity was what swayed me to baseball. The chances of getting hurt playing football are too great."

Repeatedly, Thomas was compared to Jackson, but he never felt he was of the same caliber. He felt football was Jackson's best sport and baseball was his.

Thomas was stung when he sat by the phone for three days waiting for someone to call, but was not chosen by a Major League team coming out of high school. After his junior year at Auburn, the White Sox made Thomas a first-round draft pick and paid him a bonus in six figures. Sometimes sportswriters and teammates made fun of Thomas for knowing all of his hitting statistics and comparing himself to other league leaders, but to Thomas the numbers served as validation that he was worthy of the attention others were getting. The snubs of the past stayed in the back of his mind.

Thomas made strong first impressions during his minor-league stops and made his Major League debut in 1990 with a 60-game call-up—straight from AA, bypassing AAA—starting in August. In his mind it was a case of what-took-you-so-long. And since he hit .330, it was a valid point.

THE SETTING

It took less than two months for Frank Thomas to establish himself in the White Sox lineup. It took less than two months for Thomas to demonstrate he had the goods to become a future White Sox great. The only thing wrong with those two months was that he played too much to qualify as a rookie of the year candidate for 1991.

That year, on the roster for the whole season, Thomas batted .318, hit more than 30 home runs and drove in more than 100 runs. He showed a phenomenal batting eye and worked even the best pitchers for walks. Within a few seasons, Thomas was being talked about as a potential all-time great, as possibly the greatest player in White Sox history and, along with Ken Griffey Jr., one of the finest ballplayers of his Major League generation.

Thomas was engaging with the media, was always a threat in disrupting the opposition when he stepped to the plate, and was the player fans and foes thought of first when they reviewed the White Sox lineup. For fans it was because he was popular and productive. For foes it was because they had to devise strategies to pitch around him or risk being beaten. Thomas was only 23, but he demonstrated the approach of a seasoned hitter right away, being very selective about the pitches he swung at instead of flailing with a big swing and being fooled.

"What he's got going for him is he's got a pretty good idea of the strike zone at the plate," said veteran teammate Carlton Fisk. "Most big hitters don't have that good sort of patience, or the kind of discipline at the plate he seems to have."

For most of the 1990s, Thomas was a superior player, an All-Star who was among the American League leaders in all hitting categories. He won two most valuable player awards and was a 10-time .300 hitter. He hit a blip in 1998 and 1999 when things soured in his marriage (leading to divorce and separation from his three children), the business he founded ran into problems, and his big body suffered a few cracks. It was a tumultuous time and it suddenly seemed as if the world had turned against him and forgotten all of the good things he had done on the field and for charities.

At times, Thomas ill-advisedly lashed back and was abruptly criticized in the sports pages and among fans. For a sensitive man with a lot on his mind, it was a stunning reversal. Thomas spent the off-season rebuilding his mind and body and retooling for another shot at greatness. It worked. The 2000 regular season was one of Thomas' finest. He batted .328 with 43 home runs and 143 RBIs. Anybody who had suggested that he was on the downside of his career had to keep quiet.

Thomas played 16 seasons with the White Sox and had more memorable games than he can count. He played on many good teams, but not so often that the Sox could take the playoffs for granted. In 2000, in mid-September, Chicago was close to wrapping up the Central Division title. The Sox were 86-57 when they met the Detroit Tigers at Comiskey Park.

THE GAME OF MY LIFE
BY FRANK THOMAS

CHICAGO WHITE SOX VS. DETROIT TIGERS, SEPTEMBER 11, 2000

I had so many great games with the White Sox for so many years, it's hard to say that one stands out above all of the others. There were many great moments for me in Chicago. But there was a game late in the season that I remember. We were pushing for the playoffs. The team had a lot of momentum.

I hit a home run late in the game and we won it. It didn't decide the pennant, but it made us feel like we were going to win it. We had a lot of hopes for the team that year. I can still remember that a lot. It was a wonderful time and it's something I'll always remember.

GAME RESULTS

The White Sox beat the Tigers 10-3 before 21,527 fans at Comiskey Park and increased their lead in the standings to eight games. They eventually won out over Cleveland by five games.

Thomas was 2-for-5 at the plate in the game with five RBIs. He doubled in the first inning, but the big blow was his grand slam in the eighth inning off Detroit pitcher Nelson Cruz. Thomas didn't say so, but the big hit, the big win, and the roll the White Sox were on were especially satisfying coming off two seasons of uncertainty and disappointment. The White Sox clinched the division title 11 days later to advance to their first postseason play in seven years, but lost in the American League Division Series in three straight games to the Seattle Mariners.

As the years passed in Chicago, Thomas became more entrenched as an elder statesman who was moving up the all-time team lists in the record book just about every time he stepped to the plate. But as so often happens with aging players who have stayed with one team their whole career, Thomas suffered injuries that made the team wonder about his future. His contract ended and was disputed in public, and there was another backlash against Thomas when his angry comments about his relationship with the Sox were reported in the media.

Worse, Thomas had to deal with two stress fractures to his left ankle that sidelined him for months at a time, raising the issue of whether he could play at all anymore. When Thomas was slumping and not hitting to the standards he had established, he took some fan abuse. When the White Sox met the Chicago Cubs in an inter-league series Thomas was taunted by Cubs fans wearing T-shirts with the message, "The Big Skirt" on them. It got on his nerves.

At the same time, baseball was being engulfed in a shameful scandal where it became obvious, with increasing documentation, that many of the successful players of the 1990s used steroids to help them set personal bests. Thomas, blessed with a magnificent physique, might have been suspect, but he steadily and repeatedly over the years took public stands against the use of performance-enhancing drugs. When a Congressional committee convened hearings in 2005, Thomas was eager to put his thoughts on the record. Under oath, Thomas said he never took steroids and said he thought children should be educated about their evils.

REFLECTING ON BASEBALL

During the White Sox run to the 2005 World Series championship, Thomas missed the first chunk of the season recovering from one ankle surgery. Then he came back, hit 12 homers in 34 games, helped the team when it was slumping, and reinjured the ankle, necessitating another surgery. As the Sox swept to the crown, Thomas could not play. But he *had* contributed when healthy, and celebrated with his teammates when the World Series ended in Houston and again with the fans when the city threw a parade.

It was a high note, but after that Thomas was gone from Chicago, allowed to leave as a free agent. The timing of Thomas' ankle problems, coupled with the end of his contract, left general manager Kenny Williams in a difficult position. He did not feel that he could count on Thomas to be his full-time designated hitter anymore. Once Williams decided he no longer trusted Thomas' health, he traded for Jim Thome.

Thomas was out of luck with the Sox, but he was not out of luck with baseball. The Oakland Athletics signed Thomas to a one-year deal and he still had plenty left, bashing 39 homers and driving in 114 runs. After that season Thomas signed a two-year contract with Toronto.

In late June of 2007, Thomas reached a notable career milestone while in a Blue Jays uniform, swatting his 500th home run against the Minnesota Twins. He felt great satisfaction in that moment and although some skeptics said the value of 500 home runs had been diluted by certain players using steroids, Thomas felt quite the opposite and explained his emotions on a team visit to Chicago.

"I don't want to hear people talking about that anymore when they're a true 500," Thomas said. "I know it took a couple of broken ankles and everything else for me to get there, so I'm happy to be there. I most definitely had my doubts I would get there. The last year (in Chicago) was a trying year, but I worked my butt off and came back stronger. I'm just happy to still be on my feet."

Thomas was in his 18th season. He was not as young as he used to be, but still seemed youthful. He was not thinking about retirement just yet.

"Good health is the key," he said. "I've told everybody I want to play the game until I was 41. I'm 39 and hoping I have another two strong years left. I'm 39 years old. Who knows if my Superman years are over with, but I'm still making a great contribution. I've still got a chance to have a great year. Hitting 30 home runs and driving in 100 runs, I think that's good for a 39-year-old guy."

The idea of the Hall of Fame was floated, but Thomas said it was something to think about later.

"We'll see how that works out," he said. "I think I've paid my dues so far, but I'm not done and I want to continue to work hard for the next couple of years."

Thomas said he remains on good terms with Sox owner Jerry Reinsdorf, but that he and general manager Williams don't really speak. Given the way he broadcast his feelings at the time, Thomas made no secret he felt he had been betrayed when Williams let him leave after the 2005 season.

Each time Thomas returns to U.S. Cellular Field he is greeted warmly. During his first appearance in Chicago in an Oakland uniform, the team played highlights of his White Sox career on a video board and fans gave Thomas a standing ovation. He hit two home runs in that game. In 2007, Thomas came to town with Toronto for a series and was greeted with a message on the stadium video board in the first inning, reading, "Congratulations Frank Thomas on your 500th career home run."

Thomas said he hopes that someday the White Sox will retire his jersey—such a gesture would mean a lot to him.

"Of course it would," he said. "If you go to open that book (the team media guide), you'll see my name in there quite a bit."

But that's all retirement-related stuff and Thomas remains very much in the moment of playing 162-game seasons where baseball is on his platter every day.

"My attitude and my enthusiasm are the same as they were when I was 10 years younger," Thomas said. "Every game counts for me, and at 39 I still think I can get a hit every time. I know that's not going to happen, but that fire still burns every day."

CHAPTER 27

MARK BUEHRLE

Mark Buehrle grew up in Missouri rooting for the St. Louis Cardinals. He had a Cardinals poster on the wall of his bedroom as a young fan and once, during his time with the White Sox, in answering a reporter's question he implied that he wouldn't mind playing for the hometown team one day. The comment set off a hullabaloo and the moment of candor dogged Buehrle. Years have passed, a contract has run out, a new one has been signed, and he is still in Chicago.

The left-handed pitcher had an all-American upbringing in St. Charles, Illinois, in a closely knit family. One of four children raised by John and Pat Buehrle, he got his baseball initiation there, played Little League, and learned to appreciate the outdoors, one of his strongest passions. John Buerhle was a water systems manager in St. Charles, Missouri, for 29 years. Buehrle was a Boy Scout (some people think he still is) and played some kind of sport whenever he could, from backyard football to organized baseball, yet for all of his success, he developed a modest persona.

As a youngster, Buehrle was good enough to do well playing with other kids. But when he entered Francis Howell North High School, he stood only 5-foot-4. While Buehrle had excellent control on the mound, he did not make a physical impression and ended up getting cut from the team in both his freshman and sophomore years. For years Buehrle thought he would become a baseball player, so he could

197

have been crushed by the decisions, in part because of a coach's poor judgment and administrative mistakes.

Buehrle had always played for fun, not glory, so he kept playing baseball with friends and on summer teams. Outwardly, Buehrle took the disappointment of not making the school team pretty well, but he almost didn't go out again as a junior. His father convinced him it was worth the trouble.

Blossoming in his final two years of high school, Buehrle still didn't have scouts salivating. Not a 95-mph fastball thrower, his skills are better appreciated upon repeated viewing. He enrolled in Jefferson College and got better and better. One day Buehrle walked off the field after a game and scouts handed him some information cards. He thought they were joking, but by then he had grown to 6-foot-2 and when the White Sox picked him in the 38th round in 1998, Buehrle signed for $187,000.

Buehrle owns a house not far from the one he grew up in and has told his brothers and old friends that if he ever comes home acting in a big-time, showboating manner, it is their job to belt him upside the head and remind him who he is.

There have been times on home visits when the Cardinals were in the playoffs and the White Sox were not, that Buehrle and pals have sat in the stands in St. Louis to watch games. He goes in quasi-disguise, mostly meaning he pulls a baseball cap low over his eyes and avoids recognition. Buehrle's ego is still apparently only the size of a baseball when he's away from the field. That doesn't mean it isn't big enough to pitch winning baseball for the Sox, however.

THE SETTING

If Buehrle was a late bloomer compared to some Major League pitchers, he made up for it by rushing through the minors. In 1999, Buehrle pitched in 20 games at Burlington of the Midwest League. In 2000, before he was called up, he went 8-4 with a 2.28 earned run average for Birmingham in the Southern League. Every time you put the kid Buehrle out on the mound, you had a chance to win. Sure enough, in 28 appearances for the parent club in 2000, Buehrle went 4-1.

After that season, Buehrle became a regular member of the rotation and for the next seven consecutive years his win total was in double figures, with a high of 19 wins in 2002. He became one of the most reliable starters in the American League, always good for 200-plus innings a season and often much more. He found himself selected for All-Star teams and regarded as a no-nonsense thrower.

Buehrle does not dilly-dally on the mound. When he gets the return throw from the catcher, he is ready to pitch. He takes few breaks between pitches and regularly delivers within 12 to 15 seconds. Because of this habit, baseball people know that when it is Buehrle's scheduled turn to pitch, the game might end in two hours, 10 minutes, or less. Just as he made his way earlier in his baseball life, Buehrle does not KO batters with overpowering speed. He makes them miss. He makes them lunge. He fools them. And his control is superb. Buehrle regards bases on balls with disdain. In 2004, Buehrle struck out 165 batters and walked 51 in 245 ⅓ innings.

Quietly, through his steadiness and reliability, Buehrle had established himself as the ace of a very good pitching staff that included other starters like Jon Garland and Jose Contreras. More fanfare had surrounded them earlier in their careers, but Buehrle rose to the top. By the 2007 season, fans were beginning to recognize that out of five theoretically equal starters, Buehrle was the one who could be counted on the most and the most often.

THE GAME OF MY LIFE
BY MARK BUEHRLE

CHICAGO WHITE SOX VS. TEXAS RANGERS, APRIL 18, 2007

When I see my name connected to a no-hitter, it seems unreal. You see "last no-hitter pitched in the Major Leagues" and you see my name. It's kind of overwhelming. I don't think it will sink in until the off-season when I'm at home. Maybe I'll be sitting in a tree stand when I'm out hunting deer or something like that and I'll just look back at what happened during the season.

I was the same way with the World Series in 2005. When we first won it, I don't think it hit me until I was back home and watching World Series DVDs. Watching that, it finally sort of hit me, what we just accomplished. I don't know if those things really settle in until you kind of get away from the game for a while and in your own element. That's when I think those things sink in.

I knew what was going on. I knew I had a no-hitter going. I probably was more nervous coming out of the eighth inning and going back to the ninth with the crowd going crazy. I could feel my knees shaking.

Everyone was trying to stay away from me (in the dugout, according to baseball superstition). I went up to Toby Hall in the fifth and said, "Hey, you know I have a no-hitter?" They were trying not to jinx me, so I figured I'd jinx myself.

GAME RESULTS

The White Sox beat the Texas Rangers, 6-0, and Buehrle was really only inches away from throwing a perfect game. Sammy Sosa was the only baserunner after walking in the fifth inning. Buehrle picked him off first base and faced only the minimum 27 batters.

"The perfect game would have been nice, too, but a no-hitter, I can't argue with that," Buehrle said after the game.

The game ended when Ranger Gerald Laird hit a slow grounder to third basemen Joe Crede, who scooped it up and threw him out at first. Buehrle struck out eight men on a cold April day with 25,390 fans at U.S. Cellular Field. His performance represented the first White Sox no-hitter in 16 years and the first White Sox no-hitter at home since Joel Horlen's masterpiece in 1967. When the game ended, Buehrle leapt into the arms of catcher A.J. Pierzynski, who said, "His stuff was the best I've seen in two years."

Then Buehrle was mobbed on the mound by his teammates. Cap removed, his hair matted with sweat, at one point Buehrle held the ball from the final out and tossed it up in the air and caught it.

Teammates and other baseball observers assumed Buehrle went out partying and drinking to celebrate. But his wife Jamie (whom he had proposed to in a tree stand while deer hunting) was pregnant and not drinking, so they just retreated to their Chicago area home that night.

"We went home, sat on the couch, and talked," Buehrle said. "I went outside and played with my dogs—Hungarian bird dogs—to kind of wear them down since they have to spend so much time in a cage."

Then Buehrle did what he often does after a game. He flipped on ESPN to watch the day's baseball highlights. It could have been a little bit of an out-of-body experience because he was the highlight of the day, yet Buehrle said it didn't feel all that strange.

"I always do it to catch up on the sport and see what's happened," he said.

While Buehrle was watching baseball, Jamie was on the computer and telephone answering 50 or so congratulatory messages and voicemails.

"A lot of it was from family and friends and ex-teammates," Buehrle said. "I think it was around midnight when we realized we hadn't eaten and we were both hungry. There was just so much stuff going on."

It may have been a relatively peaceful night, but when Buehrle went back to the ballpark the next day, media members surrounded him and asked to reflect on the no-hitter.

"The next day I had to do a lot of radio and TV interviews," he said. "It was like all the big radio stations and all the big TV stations. ESPN, *Baseball Tonight*, all these people wanted me to go on. I was told it was such an honor, but I'm not good with doing interviews. And after that game I went back home again."

REFLECTING ON BASEBALL

Still in the prime of his career, Buehrle's contract became an issue later in the season. He entered negotiations for a long-term deal with White Sox general manager Kenny Williams, but for a time it seemed Buehrle and the Sox were destined to split.

As that news reached fans in the midst of a disappointing season, when the White Sox were losing a lot more than people had expected, the faithful at the ballpark began lobbying for Buehrle's retention. Fans held up signs during games urging Willliams to re-sign Buehrle. Eventually, the deal got done. Buehrle received long-term security and many millions of dollars, but signed for less than he probably could have commanded on the free-agent market.

Whenever he has time, sometimes around the All-Star break in July, Buehrle races back to St. Charles to laze around the 18-acre pond on his property. He might take out a boat or just sit on shore with a fishing pole and a worm for bait, watching his bobber.

"I like to be out just to get out," he said. "Any kind of hunting, fishing, trapping, anything I can do to be out in the woods. The first thing I do after the end of the baseball season is go home, unpack, wind down, and run outside on my property, even if it's not to hunt. Just to get away from everything."

For a short while, Buehrle won't think about baseball. But he knows one day he will want to remember it all, enjoy the thoughts about what happened during his days with the White Sox, especially the no-hitter. So he has saved a souvenir glove, a bat, some balls, pictures, and ticket stubs from that day that people gave him. He plans to take those items, frame them, and create a shadow box display. Right next to it will be a second shadow box containing items from the All-Star game and the World Series.

Those decorations summarize the first several years of Mark Buehrle's Major League career. It's still too soon to tell what might happen next. Another All-Star game? Another World Series? Another no-hitter? How many more wall decorations?

CHAPTER 28

SCOTT PODSEDNIK

Scott Podsednik grew up in sagebrush Texas, in a rural area outside of a rural area. The town of West Texas, north of Waco, has about 2,700 people and nowhere is the rooting interest in Podsednik's baseball exploits stronger. A few hours from Houston in McLennan County, West Texas celebrates the homegrown athletic hero, who began playing Little League at age six and was also prom king at West High School, as an exemplar of local pride. Podsednik played baseball, basketball, and ran track in high school and received big-time scholarship feelers from the University of Texas and other schools—for track. The schools wanted him to run the 200-meter dash and hurdles. He wanted to run the bases.

A Czech settlement in cowboy territory, West Texas has not sent many athletes to stardom, so the town has claimed Podsednik for its own through all of his long struggles in the minor leagues, through his burst of glory with the White Sox in 2005, and ever since, when injuries have slowed down the premier base stealer.

"West Texas is a little town, so obviously we didn't get a lot of exposure," Podsednik said. "Just to propel myself into pro ball, I saw that as an accomplishment, coming from where I came from. Right around my junior or senior year in high school I started figuring out, just from what people told me, that I had the ability to play the game. That didn't mean I was going to make it to the big leagues. It meant I had the physical tools to be a decent baseball player. I could run. I could hit a little bit. I could play decent defense."

Podsednik, who speaks with a twang, took years to get noticed by Major League organizations who appreciated his running ability.

"Not until about 2001 did I feel like I really started catching on," he said. "I learned how to steal bases. I learned how to use my speed on the baseball field and not until then did I really think that playing in the big leagues could be a possibility."

Podsednik always stayed in touch with the town where he grew up, and the place displayed its support for him by selling Podsednik-related souvenirs and posting Podsednik boosting signs in store windows.

"Even during the grind through the minor leagues, I know they were keeping tabs on me and wondering how I was doing," Podsednik told the *Chicago Tribune* during the 2005 World Series. He joked that the town consisted of "a lot of bars, a couple of banks." But it's the kind of place that can lend perspective to a guy who takes eight years to work his way through the minor leagues. Teachers in West Texas have said they use Podsednik as an example for students to prove they can grow up and become anything they want to be.

Podsednik knew what he wanted to be, but just didn't have a good road map. He had to pay his dues in the minors before anyone gave him a chance in the majors. Among his stops before acquiring a major-league address, were the Gulf Coast League Rangers, Hudson Valley, Brevard City, Kane County, Tulsa, and Charlotte.

Podsednik made his major-league debut with the Seattle Mariners in 2001, but made his breakthrough with the Brewers in 2003. The White Sox traded for Podsednik in December of 2004, hoping his track speed could translate into wreaking havoc on the bases and run-scoring. Manager Ozzie Guillen's plan worked. When Podsednik was healthy, he set up the Sox's offense, though in late summer of 2005 he suffered a left groin injury and missed 13 games.

THE SETTING

Podsednik batted .290 with 59 stolen bases as the White Sox cruised to the American League Central Division title. Less than six weeks into the season, Guillen had proclaimed Podsednik was "the key on this team. If he gets on base, we can do a lot of different things."

Podsednik said he derived great satisfaction in stealing a base "when everyone knows I'm going. That's what I do. That's how I have to help this club."

A table setter for the big hitters in the lineup, Podsednik drove in just 25 runs all season and didn't hit a single home run. Yet when he was sidelined, the White Sox did not score as many runs. His absence showed his value, but Podsednik's recovery time had him back in full stride for the playoffs and the World Series.

When Podsednik was a little kid he was like every other kid who played baseball. He imagined scenarios where he would come to bat in the last of the ninth inning and hit the game-winning homer in the World Series. The stuff of fantasy. Veteran players feel just making it to the World Series is an achievement and an opportunity that doesn't come along every day.

"You always dream about that stuff," Podsednik said.

For three-fourths of the season, Podsednik led the majors in stolen bases. The injury was costly. He stole only five more times in the last month while he tried to get well. It was important to the White Sox to have a full-strength Podsednik around for the playoffs.

"It refuels the team to get him back," Guillen said. "It gives the team an opportunity to play the way we did in the beginning. Everyone knows how important this kid is for us because of the type of game we play."

THE GAME OF MY LIFE
BY SCOTT PODSEDNIK

CHICAGO WHITE SOX VS. HOUSTON ASTROS, OCTOBER 23, 2005, WORLD SERIES GAME 2

We were in the World Series and it was new for most of us. We won the first game against Houston and we knew the second game was a big one to get because we would have a big lead. The score was

6-6. There was one out in the ninth inning. Juan Uribe made an out and I was batting second in the lineup.

I remember telling myself, "Just reach base any way possible." If I could reach base I could try to work myself around to scoring position. Brad Lidge was pitching in relief. He throws very hard. I got ahead in the count 2-1 and I knew Brad didn't want to walk me so he was going to throw a fastball. I was sitting there looking for one pitch in one spot. Until I got to 2-1 in the count my approach was just to try to reach base. When the ball left his hand my eyes kind of got big there for a second and I put a good swing on it. I didn't miss and drove it out of the park.

Jim Thome, Jermaine Dye, Paul Konerko, Joe Crede, those guys at times, when the situation calls for it, may walk to the plate thinking, "I might get this pitch to pop out of here and put us up a run or tie the game." But even in that situation I'm not walking up to the plate looking to drive one out of the park. It's not my game. That's not what I'm here to do. I got into a hitter's count and I was looking for one pitch to drive and I got it.

GAME RESULTS

No, hitting home runs is not Podsednik's game. He hit none in the regular season. The swat made him the first player ever to hit a game-ending postseason home run following a season where he had hit none. It is a quirky claim to fame, but it does put into perspective how unlikely it was that Podsednik would win the game, 7-6, with a single swing for pitcher Neal Cotts. The 41,432 fans at U.S. Cellular Field went crazy. It was Podsednik's lone hit in the game and it felt as if his feet barely touched the ground as he ran around the bases.

"That would be by far the biggest hit of my career without any doubt," Podsednik said, "and it's gonna be tough to top. I can't think of too many situations I could be put in and hit a bigger home run than that, at the time, and the place it happened."

The White Sox walked off the field on the walk-off homer, ahead 2-0 in the World Series. They went to Houston and won the next two games to sweep 4-0 for the club's first World Series triumph in 88 years. "That was, and will be, the biggest moment of my career," Podsednik said. "Team wise, it was a magical year from start to finish."

REFLECTIONS ON BASEBALL

A few months after the World Series victory, Podsednik married his sweetheart, Lisa, and it capped an unforgettable period in his life.

"I spent so many years in the minor leagues and the World Series was the farthest thing from my mind," Podsednik said. "I was more caught up in trying to get to the big leagues, to fight my way there, to try to establish myself as a player. A World Series seemed so far away for a guy who grinded it out for so long in the minor leagues. So at the end of that season, to be facing Roger Clemes in game one of the World Series was pretty special. Then the home run. And I got married. Personally, myself, my wife, and my family will definitely look back upon that time and say, 'Wow, what a year!'"

Podsednik saved many World Series souvenirs, but none so important as trading some autographed baseballs to the person who caught his home run ball.

"I was lucky that the guy was generous enough to work out a deal with me, so I ended up getting the ball," Podsednik said of the long-shot acquisition. "The bat is hanging in Cooperstown along with some other items from the other players. But I told my wife, 'Look, I don't know if this may ever happen again. These pictures, this memorabilia, let's do something with it. Let's hang this stuff up on the wall.'"

Almost every Major League player is appreciated where he plays and where he grew up, but the attention, warmth, and feeling towards Podsednik was magnified after the White Sox won the 2005 World Series.

"The city just went crazy," Podsednik said. "To see how much the fans appreciated what we had accomplished and to celebrate with those guys during the parade and other times was just indescribable."

Then Podsednik made a pilgrimage to West Texas. He made speeches, was presented with awards, and signed autographs.

"It gave me a chance to cheer about 2005 with some of those guys," Podsednik said. "I fielded questions and talked. It's fun to go back and share those memories and get to relive all of that stuff."

Podsednik's luck with the White Sox did not run so well since the World Series. He suffered several injuries that hobbled him and stole his running game, and it is unclear if he will remain with the team. For someone who had to work so hard to make it to the majors and have the opportunity to shine on the national stage, Podsednik is not ready to give up the game and after the 2007 season he joined the Colorado Rockies.

"It all boils down to attitude," he said of how he hung in for years. "It boils down to how badly you want something, I think. If you want something badly enough, you're pretty much willing to make the sacrifices and you're willing to do whatever it takes to get to that level. I told myself around 2000, 'Look, I have the ability to get there, and I'm not going to stop until I break in.' Unless they kicked me out of the game and said, 'You're not good enough to play,' I was going to give it everything I had to at least try to get to the big leagues. Ultimately, it worked out."

CHAPTER 29

BOBBY JENKS

Bobby Jenks started playing Little League baseball in California when he was about 10 years old and he just loved the game.

"For me, it was always baseball," Jenks said. "From the time I started playing, it was just everything I wanted to do."

He and his brother played baseball as often as they could, but they were not influenced by older family members. Jenks' father's favorite sport is NASCAR racing.

"He's still a NASCAR guy," Jenks said. "My younger brothers were both great athletes when they were young, but they didn't have it—the drive—maybe as much as I did. I kind of broke off and followed my dream."

After Jenks' family moved to Washington, he participated in sports at Inglemoor High School in Bothell, a Seattle suburb, where he caught the eye of the California Angels' scouting staff. They liked his size and velocity. Jenks flirts with 100 mph on the radar gun. As so many young hurlers do, however, he needed to learn how to harness his firepower and develop into a pitcher rather than simply a thrower. During Jenks' first summer in pro ball in 2000, when he was only 19, he played for Butte in the Pioneer League. His rawness was still evident when he led the rookie league in walks and losses. It would have been hard to imagine that at 24 Jenks would be a starring actor in the deciding game of the World Series.

The years in between were not easy for Jenks. As he shifted between minor-league assignments, he had almost continuous, career-interrupting arm miseries, and at a stop or two his off-field behavior was deemed questionable. Bringing beer onto the bus and engaging in a fight with a teammate can get a player branded as a troublemaker.

In Cedar Rapids, Arkansas, and Salt Lake City, Jenks went on the disabled list four times in three years with shoulder strain, elbow strain, and elbow irritation—all in his throwing arm. After the 2004 season, the White Sox claimed Jenks on waivers anyway. A combination of maturity and good health meshed to transform Jenks' prospects in 2005 after an impressive half-summer in AA Birmingham. The White Sox did not need a closer. They were set and happy with Dustin Hermanson, who compiled a 2.04 ERA with 34 saves as the Sox positioned themselves for a first-place division finish and a run through the playoffs. If anything, Jenks looked like a potential insurance policy to beef up the bullpen.

THE SETTING

Things were sailing along smoothly for the White Sox. They were creating excitement in Chicago. Manager Ozzie Guillen had the team playing "Ozzie Ball," and the pitching staff was outstanding—starters, middle relievers, and closer included.

Until Hermanson got hurt. Suddenly, the brutal truth was that the entire season might be riding on the previously iffy right arm of a player nobody knew much about. A complete stranger to the fans, with no Major League track record, Jenks stepped in as closer to close the regular season and did well immediately. Jenks won the hearts of fans with his somewhat chubby build, his youthful face, his rocket-like fastball, and his shut-'em-down results. In 32 games, Jenks recorded a 2.75 ERA. Hermanson had been the man and no one relished the idea of going into the playoffs without him, but the presence of Jenks meant that there was no need to panic.

As the White Sox sought to fight off the late-season charge of the Cleveland Indians to clinch the division crown, it gradually became known that Jenks had not been a game closer very long—his only experience as a closer was in Birmingham. And suddenly he was asked to be the cornerstone of the White Sox bullpen in a pennant race. No pressure. Jenks could either live with a meltdown that might cost him his career, or he could rise to the occasion and carry the team on his shoulders. He was at the crossroads of opportunity and washout.

"There is no consolation prize right now," pitching coach Don Cooper said as the season wound down.

Jenks came through. The team and fans rallied behind him. He carved out a niche, making fantasies of his childhood come true. The White Sox won the division, won 98 games, and cruised into the playoffs on a high. And because Jenks was 6-foot-3, 275 pounds, sometimes Guillen walked out of the dugout to make a pitching change using his hands to make an arc—as in, "give me the big guy"—instead of tapping his right arm to signal that the righty Jenks was being summoned. It took only a few outings for Jenks to transform worry into confidence. When fans saw him enter a game, rather than fret about the arrival of a rookie whose name they didn't know three months earlier, they sighed in contentment. They felt Bobby would bail them out.

As the regular season ended and the playoffs were set to start, a sportswriter noted Jenks sitting around the Sox clubhouse wearing a T-shirt reading "Mission October." The writer also spotted a tattoo of a demon on Jenks' right thigh. Maybe Jenks wasn't all that innocent. Maybe he knew what he was all about. Closers need a killer instinct. They must have a no-mercy outlook. And they must bring it every day. Between the size of his body and the speed of his fastball, Jenks could intimidate a batter.

By the time the first round of the playoffs began against the Boston Red Sox, fans roared every time Jenks hit 97 mph on the speed gun and racheted cheers up one more notch if he hit 100. They had almost completely forgotten about Dustin Hermanson. Jenks got the save when the White Sox clinched the division title. He helped the White Sox power past the Red Sox and the Angels. Jenks seemed to constantly wipe sweat from his brow, but he never looked worried doing it.

"Nothing fazes him," said then-teammate Aaron Rowand. "He's unflappable."

By the time the season culminated in the fourth game of the World Series, on the cusp of the White Sox' first championship in 88 years, it was more comforting than surprising that Jenks was on the mound.

THE GAME OF MY LIFE
BY BOBBY JENKS

CHICAGO WHITE SOX VS. HOUSTON ASTROS, OCTOBER 26, 2005

We were ahead 1-0 when I came into the game. There was nothing unusual about that. I was always coming into close games during the season. Of course I was aware that there was a little bit more at stake this time.

I started the ninth inning and they were making a lot of noise at Minute Maid Park. This was their last chance. I gave up a hit, but I tried not to let that bother me even after they sacrificed the runner to second. After Juan Uribe made that great catch falling into the stands, there were two outs. Orlando Palmeiro hit a ground ball to Uribe at short and when he threw him out at first we won. The last pitch was a curveball. I threw that well throughout the Series. I got a ball from the game. Not the last one, but I have a game ball from that game.

It's just one of those things where you don't know what you're doing because you're so happy. It's a reaction. It's a celebration. I jumped up in the air and hugged A.J. Pierzynski. It's such a whirlwind when that moment happens. It's been in the back of your mind so long that you think, "Is it real? Is it really over? Did we just do it?" That's when all hell breaks loose on the field and everybody goes crazy.

It didn't even feel like my feet touched the ground on the field. But I did come down. After I let go of A.J., Joe Crede was right there and we had big hugs and jumps and stuff. We got bowled over by the rest of the guys, so I'm laying on the ground on top of Crede with guys on top of me. It's one of those moments where it's perfect. Afterwards, because it happened so quickly, I had to go back and watch the DVD. It was wild.

GAME RESULTS

The White Sox won the game 1-0. Starter Freddy Garcia, who pitched seven shutout innings, got the win. Jenks collected the save. The 42,936 fans in Houston, who had witnessed the first World Series in Texas, got very quiet while the Sox got very loud.

Uribe, whose throw across the diamond to Paul Konerko at first base traveled about as quickly as Jenks' fastball, had, only moments before, made a diving, head-first catch of a foul ball into the stands that set up the denouement. Konerko held on to the ball from the last out and then presented it to White Sox owner Jerry Reinsdorf a few days later when the city threw its famous parade.

After the parade, Jenks, who still maintained his off-season home in the Seattle area, returned to the Pacific Northwest. He could blend in there and not be caught up in the post-Series hysteria engulfing Chicago. If he had walked down the street on Michigan Avenue, Jenks would have been mobbed so regularly he wouldn't have been able to shop. It was different in Washington state, where even the most ardent sports fan thought the White Sox winning the World Series was just nice.

"It wasn't bad," Jenks said. "I was nowhere near Chicago for a while, so I didn't get bombarded when I went out. People went about their business. For me it was really peaceful and I got a chance to really let it all sink in."

Jenks had moments where the image jumped into his head: "We're world champions!"

"A month later I had thoughts like that," he said. "For me, it all happened so fast, just jumping into the closer's role and finishing the Series. I needed time to process everything that happened."

REFLECTIONS ON BASEBALL

Jenks earned his way onto the White Sox roster under the most demanding circumstances, solidifying his place in White Sox lore. Come spring training 2006, it was apparent Jenks was the team's closer. Although Jenks tallied 41 saves that summer, he was more hittable. Batters clued into his stuff and he finished the season with an uncharacteristic 4.00 ERA. And although the White Sox won 90 games, they did not make the playoffs.

Jenks returned stronger than ever in 2007. He compiled 40 saves with a 2.77 ERA and was selected for the American League All-Star team. He was one of the few bright spots in an off year for a team that plummeted to last place. In some ways he was better than ever. In late summer, Jenks hit a hot streak where no opposing batter could hit safely off him. He reached the record of 41 straight outs, tying the Major League mark set by the Giants' Jim Barr in 1972. But that season he could not save his teammates.

Jenks will never forget a spectacular, historic rookie year. Besides a cherished game ball, he has what every professional athlete covets— a championship ring.

"I keep it in my secret place," Jenks kidded. "No, it's on display. Every now and then, for certain kinds of events, I'll wear it, but for everyday stuff, no."

The White Sox team of 1959 that won a pennant but did not win the World Series, is still appreciated by Sox fans with good memories. The fond memories of the 2005 season will probably live on even longer. Twenty or 30 years from now fans will likely still talk with special feeling about the World Series champions of 2005 and how a young man fresh from the minors helped lead them to the promised land.

CHAPTER 30

OZZIE GUILLEN

Ozzie Guillen was born in the Venezuelan town of Ocumare del Tuy, in 1964 with the given name of Oswaldo. His mother Violeta was a school principal and transferred to Los Teques when he was 11, a fortuitous move for Guillen. Venezuela has a grand tradition of producing All-Star-caliber shortstops, and Luis Aparicio's uncle Ernesto played a role in developing many of the earliest success stories. First came Chico Carrasquel, who made his name with the White Sox. He was pushed out by Hall of Famer Aparicio, who also became a star with the White Sox. Davey Concepcion, an eight-time All-Star with the Cincinnati Reds, was in his prime when Guillen was growing up and was the one he admired most because he saw him play.

In Venezuela, baseball is king. The country is mad for the sport and reveres its stars. Guillen began playing when he was five years old and for years he was a bit undersized. Even when he reached professional baseball, he had only a 28-inch waist.

For decades, Major League middle infielders, shortstops, and second basemen were the smallest guys on the field. But that is no longer true. Larger men with more pop in their bats, players like Alex Rodriguez and Nomar Garciaparra, have found a niche at shortstop in recent years. When Guillen, who was initially signed by the San Diego Padres, was coming up, the little guy could still sneak through, but the focus was changing. "I was confident with what I could do," he said. "I didn't know what they wanted me to do. I was afraid teams wanted to find a guy with bigger size, who was a better athlete. I was the opposite. I am not the guy who has the best athletic ability, but I was a baseball player. I know how to play the game, how to win baseball games."

Guillen was still self-assured, convinced that his fielding skill and hustle would earn him a chance. He was small, but certain he would succeed.

"There is one thing about baseball in my country," Guillen said. "It is the game we grow up with. We don't grow up watching anything else. Watching baseball everywhere, they're our heros. The game is important to us and maybe that helps make a difference."

The nation's love affair with the sport encompasses the entire game, but given the fabulous history at the position, a special admiration is reserved for acrobatic fielding Venezuelan shortstops.

"They would be the biggest heroes," Guillen said. "Unfortunately, I couldn't see Aparicio play. But I did have the opportunity to grow up watching Davey Concepcion, and that was the guy I wanted to be. I was a big-time Cincinnati Reds Machine fan and I wished I could one day be like him."

When he was 16, Guillen began playing in the Venezuelan winter league, where he was managed by Aparicio himself. The older man was tough on Guillen, trying to develop his skills. To improve, Guillen came to the ballpark more than five hours before games to take grounders.

THE SETTING

All of a sudden, Guillen was like Concepcion. He was the starting shortstop for a Major League team, picked up by the White Sox in the trade that sent pitcher LaMarr Hoyt to San Diego.

Always a chatterbox (he talked to teammates, opponents, umpires, and fans during the games), always a fun guy to be around, a jokester and a prankster, Guillen was immediately popular with the

White Sox and their fans (he said he wanted to have his own TV talk show).

When Guillen joined the team during the winter of 1984-85, the Sox were coming off a losing season. It was not clear if the club was moving in the right direction, or if the jobs of general manager Roland Hemond and manager Tony La Russa were safe. The deal that brought Guillen to Chicago—in retrospect a terrific one—was criticized at the time. Hoyt was coming off a disappointing 13-18 year, but he was only two seasons removed from his Cy Young Award year. Many thought the Sox were giving up on him too quickly.

The dynamics of that situation meant little to Guillen. His dream of playing big-league ball was about to come true. When the White Sox broke camp from spring training, it was clear Guillen was going to be the regular shortstop. And when the White Sox opened the 1985 season on the road against the Milwaukee Brewers, Guillen was in the lineup for the first of 150 games he played that season. No matter what happens in their careers, Guillen believes players should all choose their first game in the majors as their favorite one.

"It's the one you never forget," he said. "That's the one where whenever you talk to a player, they're going to remember that one first."

THE GAME OF MY LIFE
(AS A PLAYER)

BY OZZIE GUILLEN

CHICAGO WHITE SOX VS. MILWAUKEE BREWERS, APRIL 9, 1985

The first game, I remember it was really cold for opening day in Milwaukee. Tom Seaver was pitching for us, and it gave him the record for pitching the most opening days in the history of baseball. It was cold, but that was fine because I was excited. I had been working hard to make it. I think that day for me was special because sometimes I never thought I was going to play at that level. I was a pretty good ballplayer, but my hitting was limited. You know I didn't have any power. I wasn't a great runner. I don't fly.

I had so many thoughts that day. I said, "I'm already here. Now the most difficult thing is to stay." I got my first hit in the game. I went 1-for-5. I got a bunt base hit late in the game.

I was going crazy trying to get my wife, Ibis, and my only kid at the time, Ozzie Jr., to fly to Milwaukee from Sarasota after spring training so they could have the opportunity to see my first game. Unfortunately, it was so cold that my wife couldn't make it. Ozzie Jr. was a baby and he was too little for the cold. He didn't even have a sweater. I was worried about my kid being comfortable and I was worried about me. I felt I had accomplished what I could, to do what I should do. I spent all of my money calling my family and everybody at home in Venezuela.

None of the guys said anything about it being my first game, but Tony La Russa said, "Don't change anything. Play the way you played in the minor leagues and then you don't have to worry about anything else."

I was calm. I wasn't nervous. I was anxious. I never thought I was going to be starting with Tom Seaver pitching. It was all so exciting and shocking because I could see my dream come true. I said, "Wow, the hard work paid off."

GAME RESULTS

The opening-day crowd at County Stadium was huge, with 53,027 in attendance. The White Sox won 4-2 and Seaver picked up the victory. Guillen batted lead off, starting a new era for the Sox at shortstop. He made a solid impression around the league and made his boss Hemond very happy. People stopped talking about losing Hoyt in the trade.

"Wherever I went to speak during the season and since the end," Hemond said after Guillen won the rookie of the year honor, "people have told me he reminds them of Luis Aparicio. You can't say anything finer about him than that."

THE SETTING

After his lengthy playing career, Guillen stayed in baseball as a coach. His prominence as third base coach for the Marlins, coupled with his long history with the White Sox, made him an appealing candidate when general manager Kenny Williams sought a new manager for the 2004 season.

Guillen immediately infused the team with fresh enthusiasm, cracked jokes, told stories, kept morale strong, and despite occasional controversial statements that drew unwanted attention, was a popular and visible leader. He was a hot new property. Becoming the first Venezuelan Major League manager enhanced Guillen's status back home tremendously. His charm and out-spokenness had U.S. reporters—including *Playboy* magazine for its signature interview— lining up at his clubhouse office door.

Playboy said that Sox owner Jerry Reinsdorf referred to Guillen as "the Hispanic Jackie Mason." Guillen criticized players with a rare bluntness. He admitted throwing up in his office after losses he couldn't stomach. He made bold moves on the field that were easy to second-guess, though most of them worked out. Most importantly, under Guillen's tutelage, the Sox became winners and marched to the 2005 World Series title. The one thing he wanted to do as a player, but couldn't, was win it all. As a leader, Guillen ended the team's World Series drought and basked in the applause, cheering, and adulation of millions of Chicagoans on that day.

THE GAME OF MY LIFE
(AS A MANAGER)

BY OZZIE GUILLEN

CHICAGO WHITE SOX VS. HOUSTON ASTROS, OCTOBER 26, 2005, WORLD SERIES GAME 4

The team played so well in the playoffs against Boston, the Angels, and the Astros, and we were at the fourth game where we could win it all and win it for everybody. Nobody thought we were going to be as special a team as we were. My kids were near me during the last hour that night and I told my kids, "Finally, we do something right. We did it for the city and for Jerry Reinsdorf. Finally, the city has a championship team."

Thank God I was the manager of the White Sox when it happened, because I felt that I was a big part of this organization for all my life. I just thank God for giving me the opportunity to have that moment. I would die if somebody else was managing or coaching or playing and I wasn't part of that night.

It was a second chance. I think it's different when you imagine the World Series when you're playing. When you're playing, you enjoy it a little more because you can do something to help the team win. The manager can just enjoy the work the players do. I told the team I was glad and blessed by God that I was running the ballclub and bringing the championship to Chicago.

A lot of people said I would jump around the field. The players looked like kids, like elementary school kids. There was nothing to make me feel prouder than I was in that five minutes, or whatever it was, when I just looked at the team celebrating. It felt like 10 days and I was thinking that hard work really did pay off. I was looking at those guys having fun, celebrating, and feeling proud. I think I was the most proud man on the Earth.

GAME RESULTS

The White Sox won 1-0 to complete the Series sweep of the Astros. During the huge parade engulfing downtown city streets, Guillen was photographed holding up the championship trophy in a blizzard of confetti. Guillen often thinks about the moment when the team finished off Houston.

"Every day I can look back and remember and see Joe Crede jumping into Bobby Jenks' arms," Guillen said. "They all ran by me from the dugout. I looked at my coaching staff and see them hugging each other. I don't think I will ever forget that because we did it as a family. Harold Baines, Greg Walker, and Joey Cora, we had been together for so many years. We felt like we were young kids again. We were Jerry's kids. I think it's something that makes you feel even better about it because we grew up together in the White Sox organization as players and what we got to go through as manager and coaches was pretty great. It was awesome."

REFLECTIONS ON BASEBALL

A year after winning the World Series, the White Sox played well enough to win 90 games, but didn't make the playoffs. In 2007, the season went haywire and the team finished 72-90. Despite his continuing popularity in Venezuela—meeting with President Hugo Chavez—and his ties to his native country, Guillen, his wife, and his son Oney were sworn in as U.S. citizens on Ozzie's 42nd birthday in the fall of 2006.

Sometimes Guillen remained a provacateur, saying the first thing to come to mind. While the entire city was looking forward to the annual White Sox-Cubs match-up Guillen announced he would just as soon play the cross-town rival in a completely different part of the world. He does not like the massive amount of attention that comes with the games.

"Swear to God, next year we're going to play the opening Cubs-White Sox series in Japan," Guillen said during the spring of 2007.

Escaping the country looked great to him as the season frayed. He just wanted to go somewhere for a vacation where no one would recognize him and talk baseball. Maybe Antarctica, it was suggested. No, Guillen said. In the end, when the Sox finished miserably and his customary energy and enthusiasm were waning, Guillen figured out where to head to recharge his batteries and ponder the 2008 season. When the 2007 baseball season ended, Guillen fled to Spain. There wasn't a designated hitter in sight.